THE WAY

T. Michelle Jacobs

Copyright 2012 T. Michelle Jacobs

All rights reserved.

ISBN-10: 0615737293
ISBN-13: 978-0615737294

DEDICATION

This book is dedicated to my son, Jacob Charles

CONTENTS

~ACKNOWLEDGEMENTS~

~PREFACE~

~INTRODUCTION~

~THE WAY~

~THE DISHEVELED NATURE OF GLORIA TYNE~

~THREE~

~PEACE OF ME~

~RAIN~

~GRATEFUL~

ACKNOWLEDGEMENTS

Thank you to my parents for your love and confidence in me. Kelvin, thank you for your love and for taking such good care of me. I love you and because of your help, I have the time to write. Thank you to all of my family for your love and support. So much love to my 'besties', Stacy, Tonia, Temieka, Jessica and Michelle, my team and partners. You lift me up and believed in me even when I didn't believe in myself. Thank you to Michelle Phillips for your photography for all of our projects. Thank you to Winston-Salem Writers for your inspiration. I would like to express my appreciation and love for my family and friends in the neighborhood where I grew up in Winston-Salem, NC. You inspire me.

The author of this book does not dispense medical advice or prescribe the use of any technique as a form of treatment for any physical, emotional or medical problems without the advice of a physician, indirectly or directly. This publication is meant to be inspirational and entertainment. In the event that you use any of the information in this

book for yourself, the author assumes no responsibility for your actions.
T. M. Jacobs/PIP

PREFACE

    For as long as I can remember words have been my friends. When I was lonely, afraid, confused and even happy, I used words on paper to express myself. I found that I had the ability to express myself in ways that were empowering and freeing even if I was the only one that read them. My love for and exposure to music at an early age nourished my appreciation for words. I was always musically inclined and was always involved in band or chorus. Dissecting melodies and lyrics was fun to me and meaningful.

    As I got older I began to discover the real power of words, verbalized or written; how someone being callous and cold with them could be hurtful yet someone speaking kindly had the reverse affect. Humor has a way of healing as well. Humorous words can make you smile inside. Learning to laugh, even through pain is good for the soul. So many things have happened, some good. some wonderful, some bad and some horrible, as with everyone. I have loved, been loved, fallen in love, been hurt, been happy and content, discontented and miserable but through it all I still remain in love with words.

    I love to write. I especially love writing poetry. Poetry to me is simply writing with rhythm, something I think I learned from my love of music and lyrics. I like to tell stories with poetry, stories that empower, enlighten and inspire. Even if you do not love poetry I think that you will enjoy this book because there is a familiarity with all of us that excels preference and indulgence and that is the heart. Love, pain, sickness, pleasure , desire, need and struggle affect us all. The only difference is the way we feel about it, the way we deal with it and the way we inspire others. I sincerely hope that you are inspired.
T. Michelle Jacobs

INTRODUCTION

    Life has a way of revealing what is true. The truth is neither complex nor

intricate. It simply is. The value is in the realization that everyone has their own truth, what it was, what it is. Some people carry secrets so deep within them that they can not find them. All of us have suffered loss and tragedy in some
form. Something as minor as being unknowingly overlooked to being intentionally, severely mistreated can be traumatic to our hearts and our minds. Some of us carry deep scars and unfortunately many of us have kept secrets from childhood that no child should have to experience or even worse, hold inside. When we were children we learned the refrain 'sticks and stones may break my bones but names will never hurt me', but the truth is, words do hurt. They can pierce like needles or cut deeply leaving wounds. Attacks are not always physical, they can be verbal as well. Definition of Attack: to set upon in a forceful, violent, hostile or aggressive way, with or without a weapon; to begin hostilities against; start an offensive against; to blame or abuse violently or bitterly; to direct unfavorable criticism against; criticize severely; argue with strongly.

    Words can hurt. But just as words can hurt they can heal. Just think about skilled surgeons. They use instruments that can easily be used to hurt someone but they wield them skillfully, gently repairing damage made by any weapons. Similarly, words can be lovingly and gingerly used to repair wounds left by weapons of anger, deceit, hate and mistreatment If tactfully and kindly presented, words can allow healing to begin. Whether it is physical or emotional abuse that one has suffered, healing words can play a part in recovering from the damage. When you have been physically hurt and a physician applies his medical knowledge to help you it also helps you emotionally, why? Because of the positivity. Knowing that you will recover feeds your hope and determination. So regardless of the origin of hurt and pain, allow words to begin your healing. Not just serious words but lighthearted, humorous words as well. Learning to laugh can be calming and soothing to the soul as well.

 Why is truth not complex or intricate? The answer can be found in the knowledge that learning never ceases. Once you have the knowledge, you know, but the process of understanding is ongoing. When something happens, it happens and there is no changing it, simple , however how it happened, why it happened even when it happened can always be debated. Whether those questions are answered or not, the fact remains that it happened. Regardless of its dimensions any negative experience will affect us in some way and every positive experience will as well. The value and the power is not in the understanding. It is in the realization.

ACCEPTANCE

Worry me no more, no longer sit at my door
No longer wait for me, my acceptance has set me free
Like rain after blistering heat, bring me back from defeat
Make me whole again, I am determined, I know I can
Soothe me with your words of softness, rock me gently to a rhythm only
My heart knows, calm the rivers of my expectations and guide my sails on the waters of my reality. Hold my hand , guide my steps until I am blind no more
Be my ears until I can hear, stop my knees from knocking and my hands from shaking by steadying my feet and shed light on my path so that even
in the dark, I can find my way

~THE WAY~

Soft light peering thru the cracks of the wall
I slowly approach cautiously objective
Brighter it gets and as my shadow appears
The outline of my outer self is unrecognizable to me
Who is hiding in the dark? My fear is

growing and my breathing shallow
Quietly I pace my footsteps as if avoiding a predator
Not making a sound I approach, anxious yet apprehensive
Cautious yet emboldened, afraid yet courageous
All that has brought me to this precipice has culminated into
A narrow escape, I'm fighting for my life
Darkness will not dissuade me, fretfulness will not mar my
Determination. Tears well in the pool of my eyes and drizzle my
Cheeks although the shower of moisture from my brow render
Them indiscriminate. I pause to slow the pounding in my chest
And kneel to avoid detection. Crouching as if preying on an
Unsuspecting victim I peek thru the fissures to catch a glimpse of the
Other side. Hope slowly fills my being from the bottom of my feet
To the tip of my head like a bottle slowly filled with warm liquid .
Too soon to be relieved I release a muffled sigh and silently breathe in, then out.
Suddenly the light becomes brighter and I'm momentarily blinded by
It's brilliance. As my eyes adjust I'm aware that I am vulnerable and my escape
Must be quick and deliberate without a guide to follow, a leap of faith.
As my vision follows the tunnel of light, I feel empowered. Thru my blackened

Surroundings, I can see, The Way.

The human heart always has hope, even if it is just the tiniest glimmer. It will continue to hope until there is no inkling of a spark. If there is one little spark, hope will hang on.

~THE DISHEVELED NATURE OF GLORIA TYNE~
Born and welcomed into the world
Aged before her awaiting years
Celebrated by those preceding her
Mother's loving sentimental tears
Nurtured talents praiseworthy goodness
Blessed with poetic endless rhyme
Curious demeanor disheveled nature
The lyrical prowess of Gloria Tyne
Running wildly crazy banter
Thoughts disarranged like books on shelves
Shining eyes alphabetized words
Tiny dutiful busied elves
Dancing around in mellow drama
Causing ruckus and raising sand
That's what Grandma said of Gloria
Willingly giving a gentle hand
Let her be for time will tell
If her abilities have troubled nerves
Giving her tonic and strange smelling water
Gardened growing bitter herbs
Prancing in circles getting dizzy
Feels so oddly soothing and normal
Sit at the feet of grandpa's stories
Imagining gatherings proper and formal
Gifts of jasmine lemon and rosemary

Baked in floured kneaded dough
Fried tomatoes that taste like meat
Steaming biscuits that she loved so
Melting butter dripping from the pan
Mesmerized by a ticking clock
Running from switches and laughing naughtily
Ending halfway up the block
Jumping rope and throwing jack rocks
Playing hopscotch in the street
Do children even play those games anymore?
Or run to the neighbors house for a treat?
Of course not, times have changed
They're all locked behind closed doors
Don't even beg to go outside
Not interested in the goings on anymore
All grown up prettier and wiser
Amazed at the time that has passed by
How did the tree outside her window
Grow so big and touch the sky?
How did the three kisses on her forehead
Float away with dreams of brooks
Babbling quietly steadily flowing
Sitting all day reading books
Teenage love and branded friendships
Drift away like wood on seas
Getting "A"s and loathing "C"s
Winning local spelling bees
Troubled mind and softened ego
Destined to dream love and believe
Angelic countenance, weakened limbs
Healthy heart that's worn on sleeve
Gloria Tyne and the lovely girls
Pretty boy with friends in tow
Time will move on and seem to evade you

> So much sooner than you know
> Headlined news and distant happenings
> Wrapped in laws and legislature
> Sum the total of Gloria Tyne
> And of her disheveled nature

As she lie on her side and braced herself thru the pain in her back, sweat running horizontally across her forehead, Gloria prayed for strength. Every morning her body wracked with pain she started her day with endurance and faith; faith that she could make it yet another day. She mentally fought to gather her thoughts and organize in her mind, the tasks of the day. Getting to her feet was the most difficult part. After that she would shower, dress, partake of her vegan breakfast and chip away at her accomplishments for the day. She called them accomplishments at the urging of her therapist. She looked forward to their weekly sessions. Psychological therapy had been a part of her life for a long time. Although off and on, it had helped to sustain her stability. She grabbed her cell phone and electronic tablet. 'I'm forgetting something', she thought. 'My purse, my key's! I'm gonna be late! I can't be late!' If her best friend El called and she wasn't out the door, she would get an earful. 'Okay take a deep breath, in and out. You got this. Calm your nerves. My notes, where are my notes?', again panicking inside. "oh, they're on my tablet! Okay calm Gloria, calm. If El was here she would say, 'Calm down, let's go.'

    She stepped out of her car impeccably dressed. A crisp white shirt under a black blazer, adjusting her favorite black skirt because of it's elegance and modest length. Adorning patent leather black heels, every step withstood with a hint of pain, the strides were worth their cost. As Gloria entered the building she was greeted and escorted to the holding room where she was briefed on radio protocol. It was all a blur; questions and answers; answers and questions; So many crammed into the passing year.

    After her interview she had plans to meet her best friend. She and El (short for Eleanor) had been friends since they were children. El was the only person in the world that knew everything there was to know about her. "Glori(El's nickname for Gloria) you did a great job this morning. Sorry I couldn't go with you." " It's ok El' you can only be one place at a time." They smiled at each other as if still children holding a secret. " I'm ready El." "You know there may be some hard questions. " I know", Glori took a sip of her tea. She had a long day ahead of her. El reminded her to give herself enough time so that her nerves wouldn't be frazzled. "Sometimes you're all over the place Glori," El would say teasingly, "but it's ok, we got this."

    From the corner of her eye she spotted El worriedly making last minute adjustments. Glori smiled to herself at the thought of El being more nervous than her. That's the way it was with them. The supporting friend was always more apprehensive than the one in the situation. They had been side by side thru many events, some humorous, some that they laughed at to keep from crying and some that just made them cry. El was a treasure to her, a companion in every sense of the word....

BEST FRIEND
Thick and thin
Short and tall
You have been there thru it all
Back and forth
Up and down
I know you'll always be around
Always there for me
My right hand
Whenever I look for you
there you stand
Before the boyfriend
After the break
Wipe the tears
Help Heal the heartache
Birth of children
Graduation
Every fathomable
Situation
There you are
I always know
If someone takes it there
We will go

Before the husband
After the divorce
Always my encouraging
Driving force
Before the downpour
After the storm
There to keep me
Safe and warm
My strong shoulder
Your caring words
My amen corner
They have some nerve
Your uh-uh sayer
Oh no he did not
Oh yes she did
Your back I got
By my side
Has my back
Help getting your life
Back on track
Friends since childhood
At times we clown
But if someone hurts you
You know I'm down
If we need to get 'em
I'll lead the way
When it comes to my friend
I do not play
If it is broken
We will mend
Yours forever
My best friend

When Gloria was a little girl, she

received a gift from her mother. It was wrapped in pretty paper covered with roses and topped with a pink bow. When she opened it she gasped. It was a jewelry box. When she opened it there stood a little ballerina and she turned as gentle music played. Gloria sat there for hours winding it again and again watching the little girl dance

.

MUSIC BOX

She twirls in her pretty lacy white tutu
Beautifully poses elegant arabesque
Wearing a Shiny white satin leotard
Sitting in the corner on my desk
I moved her to my bureau with the mirror
Because she reflected in the sunlight as she danced
Peering thru the window of my bedroom
Where the moon of midnight's sorrow often glanced
She's watched me grow up from a girl to woman
And dressed me in fake diamonds and faux pearls
She's watched me dress in lacy frocks like hers
And dab on light perfume made just for girls
She sings a lullaby when she is opened
When she is closed she hides in darkness and sleeps alone
Sometimes I would open her just to hear
Her unchained melody and repeated monotonous tone

Her hair is black and shiny long and curly
Her ballet slippers dainty pink and small
As she turns on the tips of her toes
I watch her gracefully appear to almost fall
But she glides into a delicate dancers turn
A pirouette balanced skillfully on a stand
And as she slows and the music comes to an end
I wind her and she resumes at my command
She is my comfort, my reminder that someone loves me
That I am special in my own unique yet simple way
She is my friend that serenades me in the mornings
As I awaken and dress for school everyday
Her silky home has become tattered old and faded
Her tutu dingy white and weathered well
Why is it that ballerina never grows old
Along with the stories that she could tell
She has seen me giddy and happy, excited and free
Seen me battered bruised and fretful tears of shame
She has sat there silently as I stared thru the window
As the wind thru cracks in the corners called my name
Where are you, where are you going? They would ask me
What are your hopes your aspirations and your dreams?
When you grow up will you have a little girl?
And give me to her & watch her face light

up with beams
For it seems that music box has special meaning
It is a symbol that your mommy's watching you
That she loves you cherishes your heart & will always be here
Be proud, boastful and supportive whatever you do
So dance for her ballerina twirl in your tutu
Give to her what you have always given me
Give her dances choreographed by life's sweet sorrow
Give her love and someone to look at and feel free

THE BURDEN
I've carried it on my soul and in my heart for so long
It's heavy and it's painful
It's useless and a nuisance
It's bleeding me dry and and pinning me to the ground
I'm in shackles and I don't like it
I'm restrained as if in an asylum as if I'm in prison
Waiting for someone to rescue me but no ones coming
I must free myself
It ends today

As she entered the room Gloria felt the love and support in the room. Today her attacker was to be sentenced. Her testimony had helped to get him convicted and he would be going to prison for a very long time. Any pain that she endured was worth it if others were to benefit. She tried not to let her mind wander to a negative place but the intrusion was forceful. How many children had suffered harm at the hands of a predator? How many young women and men had been terrorized and abused. In her heart she knew that there were too many to imagine and the thought made a deafening sound in her mind. 'Find that good place, flee there and remain in it's refuge, she repeated her mantra silently. 'Going to that hurtful place is no longer necessary, you have moved on.' But the physical pain triggered the emotions and there is no protection from what the brain holds hostage. One lonesome day, long ago, pinning her down, the attacker beat her mercilessly into submission, damaging her spine and leaving scars both internal and external that would never go away. Her battles with depression and anxiety were now a nuisance but bearable. She had made so much progress There were scars that no one could see and the painful mornings and labored steps were undetected by the unknowing eye. Yet they were there and they always would be.

THIS

......work is so hard
So difficult, I'm praying
That I can get it done
I must believe this is the one
Feel what I say, hear me please
Tell me what you believe
Do you believe I can, do you?
I know you have faith
None have I, I don't know why.
Return my stars to the sky
Let me hold my moon, night is my friend
I believe, No I don't believe
I'm finished with this losing game
The result is always the same
No one is to blame
Someone scream my name
I'm tired of losing, I want to win
Tell me where I need to begin
Dim the sun, allow me to hold the rain
My emptiness can hold it all
Please hold my hand lest I fall
The nearness of the end
Time is no longer my friend
If your hand should extend
I will take hold
Because I am weary and weak
These words for me speak
This no longer is, no longer will this be
This is no longer the place for me
So hard is this, so deep
I beg you my memory keep
Close to your heart where none can retrieve

If you believe, I believe

To Gloria With Love

    "Gloria, what are you feeling?" her therapist was concerned because she was unusually quiet. This was usually a safe place to release but today she was reserved. "I don't know. I just feel defeated." her expression was solemn. " Why are you feeling that way? You're not defeated. Look at how far you have come." " I know but it seems I always arrive back where I started. "Twenty years ago I wrote a letter to myself. I didn't believe a word of it but the hope was that in time, I would. I'm not sure I do yet." She reached into her purse and removed a tattered white envelope. Inside was her letter written on plain ruled notebook paper:
"Dear Gloria, your future is so bright. Nothing can stop you. You are smart, you are beautiful, you are strong. Life will take you anywhere you want to go. Love will overflow in your heart and you will always be everything that you need. You are complete. You are the answer. You are everything. When things get tough rely on your inner strength. Hold your head up high an look straight ahead. There is always something new around each corner. Follow your dreams, fulfill them and live them. And always remember that I will always be here

for you. No matter how hard it gets, I will never let you down."

"Do you believe it Gloria? You've been living as though you believe it. You're just feeling a little unsure right now." Gloria turned her head almost as if she was expecting someone else to answer. She managed to reply, " I believe it".

THE VICTOR

Taking what's mine and walking away
You tried to steal my power
Though the battle you won, you lost the war
This is your final hour
You prey on the weak, and bully the small
But the protector is strong and bold
Whatever is done in the dark of night
The story will not go untold
So cower in the corner, or face your doom
Your time will surely come
There is no place for you to hide
You darkened loathsome one
I will not wait or search for you
As you stand in shadows to evade
When your time comes there will be no haven
You cannot masquerade
The person you are will come to light
It's not my place to revile
There is a wrath for those that choose
To prey upon a child
The victory is mine because I'm alive
And I stand here beautiful and strong
You never had the weapons to win

You were beaten all along
Look up at me from your lowly place
I will always be on top
You tried to end my progression
But I will never stop
I will no longer think of you
You never existed to me
You tried to trap me within myself
But my love has set me free
I will help those who suffered the same
I'll be their guiding light
I'll shine for them thru their darkest times
And help them in the fight
The power belongs to the one who asks
And struggles for victory
You see the right thing to do
Is earn what you get
Not try to take it from me
Always remember that you never can keep
What does not belong to you
You will have to answer to a higher power
And you will receive your due
Victory is mine I will share the wealth
I carry the prize in my hand
I will not buckle under the pressure
As the victor here I stand

  Gloria had come so far, suffering with depression and battling mental and physical health issues that her injuries had caused. Her thoughts and ideas had been in disarray and her nerves were all over the place. It was extremely difficult to focus but she was always determined. This was a new start. With the past completely behind her, she could move forward. She would be starting graduate school in the fall, her favorite time of year. As she walked to her car, she stopped to look at the sky and the clouds floating by and she took a deep breath in and then out. Gloria took the letter out that she had written so many years ago once more and as if it was asking her a question she responded, " I believe."

BELIEVE
I can do anything
Because I believe
I can be anything
Because I believe
I believe that a heart can heal in time
I believe that what I desire can be mine
I believe that I will be just fine
I believe in you because you were there for me
I believe in a kind soul
I believe in a loving touch
I believe so much
I refuse to believe a lie
I will not even try to make it the truth
I will move on
And I will believe in what is real
I believe in what I feel
In my life I will help others believe
I believe in not giving up
I believe that all will be done

That needs to be done
And I will have played a part in success
Because I believe

The human heart always has hope, even if it is just the tiniest glimmer. It will continue to hope until there is no inkling of a spark. If there is one little spark, hope will hang on.

~~~~~~~~~~

~THREE~
Life is short
Life is free
What has a cost is love
Painful, blood sweat and tears they say
The truth is today
I'm doing it my way
There is no time to play
Love is an expensive rare and precious jewel
The price no monetary value can contain
Long or short sweet or bitter
Deep or shallow forceful or meek
Love is not for the weak
If the truth is what you seek
Undeniable
Unreliable
Lucid viable
Beloved yet liable
God originated
Two created
Man and woman bound to God
Bound by God

Unequivocal sun's ray
Today is the day
I must do it his way
With no words to say
May my heart convey
Graciousness have thee for
The braided cord of three

    Have your heart no sound , let it's drum pound and resound. Live inside keep your soul and hold it tight thru the night until cometh the light oh sing my heart find your voice clear your throat and sing...the morning bring. Addison's mother had recited this prayer for her at night for as long a she could remember. Tonight as she lie in bed she recited it to herself. She knew the morning would bring confrontation and she did not want to face it. She and her husband were facing divorce. Emotions were running high. Things had gone so badly. How did it become so bad? She could picture Marc sitting there smug and arrogant. How would she keep herself from being enraged. It would not be a simple task. Her husband had become someone she no longer recognized. How can someone you loved so much, turn against you and become so mean and cold? She couldn't think about it anymore or she would upset herself and she needed to rest. She closed her eyes and mumbled her prayer until she fell asleep.

    The next day Addison found herself sitting across from the man that she had once loved so deeply; honestly, A man that she still loved deeply. She knew that he still loved her as well but somehow they couldn't show it anymore. They had known each other since they were kids. Was divorce the answer? It seemed to be the only way, but there is always another way. You just have to be willing to take it. No matter how many obstacles you have to overcome, roadblocks you face or detours you must take, true love always finds a way.

TELL

Tell my heart what my tears already know
That the pain will not leave it will only grow
It will take you over take root and sprout
Overtake your lungs and squeeze the air out
It will knock you down and deliver a blow
Put you in a chokehold and wont let you go
Clog up your arteries narrow your veins
Empower your brainwaves to deliver the pains
Tell me this is not how it ends
We can't talk to each other or even be friends
There has to be a better way
to deal with this love, to make it stay
If it leaves forever, I will truly miss

It's loving touch, it's gentle kiss
I wish I had a fairytale brew
To fix the love between me and you

HELP ME
Visualize my dream
Dream of my vision
Basked in confusion
And indecision
Feel my anxiety
Bare my soul's obsession
Rolled in heartache
And open confession
Fill in my circle
That's emptied and bare
Where love used to be
No one is there
Cry for me
And give me your tears
Peer into my mind
And see my fears
Take my shoes
And walk my path
Explore my anger
And feel my wrath
Search for my happiness
And find it for me
What is the purpose
Of letting things be
Rearrange my life
Take it apart
Put it back together
Give me a new heart
But where my sadness can dwell
Help me to get rid of it

So I can be well
Release me from prison
I have served my time
Throw me a rope
And up I will climb
Out of the depths
Off despair a pain
Please grant me relief
From going insane
I am a bird
And you are a tree
Your branches provide
Rest and comfort for me
Grab hold of my captors
And run them away
Let bitter words go
And loving lips stay
Forget who I am
That used to be me
Think of my future
And who I will be
Glowing and sunny
Dazzling and funny
Lovely and light
Gorgeous and bright
Blissful and healthy
Emotionally wealthy
That's me in my dream
My vision of truth
The woman of today
The girl of my youth
I know I can get there
I believe It can be
Only if you would
Please help me

If she had known what life had in store for her Addison felt that she would have made different decisions but who doesn't feel that way? No one has the privilege of knowing what will happen; what decisions will be the right ones, which ones will be dreadfully wrong. Sometimes things seem so right when they are wrong and so wrong when they are in actuality, so right. Love, especially when you are young can feel so confusing. Relationships are hard. Marriage is hard. Something that can bring the most blissful, unbelievable feelings can also bring you the most pain and excruciating heartache. Pain that you literally feel inside, that feels like it will break you down, leaving you injured, even dead. That's how it feels, yet you try, yet again and again. The human heart always has hope, even if its just the tiniest glimmer and it will continue to hope until there is no inkling of a spark. If there is one little spark, hope will hang on.

If he had a chance to do things differently, Marc felt that he would, but the chance was gone so why bother. Addison was so fed up at this point there was no point in trying. So here they sat, ready to divorce, ready to put an end to their misery, or was it only the beginning. He had no answer. All he knew was that his heart was broken and there was nothing that anyone could say or do to repair it.

PRAY

All I have left for you is prayer
I hope that it will get you there
I'll pray for you night and day
For God to help you find your way
I hope that you pray every night
Talk to the sky to set things right
Don't forget to pray for your mother
Who loves you more than any other
Pray for those that put up with you
And excuse the thoughtless things you do
Like not returning love that's shown
Claiming you're doing it on your own
Pray for love to touch your heart
Pray for your anger to depart
Pray for humility to find your ego
And chop it all the way down to zero
Pray for selflessness to temper your pride
Pray for warmth to come inside
Pray for your coldness to find the heat
Do not your selfish acts repeat
Pray to get rid of your attitude
To stop being mean harsh and rude
You think your persona is showing power
But when faced with obstacles you cower
Pray for courage and peace of mind
Pray for the ability to be kind
Pray that you watch what you say to me
Tell the truth it will set you free
Pray that your soul can find the light
To come out of the dark and lonely night
Pray to trust and love again
Fall in love with someone that's truly your

friend
Make yourself available to those that love
you
Pray for others, your enemies too
Don't forget to ask to be forgiven
For past mistakes and sinful living
I'm praying for my own self control
Just knowing you is taking it's toll
I wish that I never met you before
I pray for God to close that door
And make me forget your hurtful ways
I pray the further I get from those days
I prayed about letting you make me upset
Your hateful words I pray to forget
I pray you get whatever you're due
I hope I never again say you
I pray that life leads you far away
And I don't think of you another day

To their surprise the mediator gave them puzzling news. She informed them that the lawyers would not be present today. She announced that she would be holding the papers for twenty days. If after the twenty days they wanted to complete the process she would, with no questions. They had one stipulation. The two of them were instructed to write love notes to each other everyday. One note each. It doesn't matter how long it is but it has to be at least three full and complete sentences. If you can't be loving and nice you must at least be diplomatic. They were to send the notes by email simultaneously each day and the next day would be a response to one another's messages. Shocked, the two were speechless, but Marc was able to eventually bring forth, one word, why? The answer was simple. You have spent years together and years apart. Nonetheless you have invested many years. Just invest twenty days into seeing if there is a possibility to save this love. Marc and Addison separated when they were younger after 10 years of marriage yet they had never officially divorced. Now after finally deciding to make their separation permanent and legal through divorce they were being asked by their mediator to give it twenty more days and to write love notes no less. Addison nodded in agreement and quietly said okay. Marc simply mumbled, whatever. These were the letters for the next twenty days:

Day: 1
Marc: Love is painful. Love is stupid. I don't need it or want it anymore

Addison: We have to figure out which way

to go. All we can do is be honest about the way we feel but we have to listen to what the other is saying. I'm not sure if I want this. I may just be opening myself up to more hurt.

THE STAND

I can't stand you
I have to sit
Whatever I felt
You ended it
I can't stand the thought
of your voice or name
Your face your soul
it's all the same
It's hard to believe
I once loved you
Now I can't stand
The things you do
You make my skin crawl
You're awful and cruel
You're mean and bitter
And think I'm a fool
I will not stand
For your disrespect
Any kindness in you
I can't detect
Maybe it's there
But I couldn't care less
My connection to you
Has made a mess
I thought you were worth it
Now I know you're not

Your wounded ego
Is all you've got
You're sullen and broken
And refuse to repair
Your damaged parts
From wear and tear
You sit and wallow
In your misery
You tried to make
A fool of me
But you're the one that's foolish
And fake
Couldn't be a nice person
For your own life's sake
You hurt people along the way
You thought you knew everything
You had your say
Now it's my turn
You're thankless and crude
Vile, mean
Hateful and rude
Whatever you get
You dished it out
Now you're getting it back
The misery and doubt
I stand empowered
You can hurt me no more
I found the way
To go out of that door
Into freedom
Away from you
Not even memory
Want nothing to do
With your egotistical
condescending self
I put that book

back on the shelf
I don't want to read
It ever again
That story was ending
When it began
I'm so much better
Than you ever
Deserved
All you cared was that
Your needs were served
Now I'm on top
My honor at hand
In spite of you
Here I stand

Day 2
Marc: I care about you. I know you care about me. Lets just leave it at that.

Addison: Marc, I'm hurting so much inside. I want to love you but I can't find you anymore. You make me so angry because you cause so much hurt and you don't seem to be aware of anyone else's but your own. There was a time that I thought you could do no wrong , which I admit was foolish and naive on my part but now I know better. I am no longer that foolish girl that was blindly in love with you.

MY APPRECIATION
I want to thank you for letting me see
That you never really cared about me

Thank you for showing me the truth
About the person I loved in my youth
Thank you for helping me discover
That I should have listened to my mother
Thank you for being a jerk
So that I could see we would never work
Thank you for saving me
From a lifetime of hurt and misery
Thank you for bringing me to reality
that it wasn't the love I wanted it to be
I was so foolish to think that a liar and a cheat
Could somehow make my life complete
But I sincerely have to give you credit
The way you behaved I will never forget it
You helped me come back to my senses
With no hidden meanings or false pretenses
You showed me that you never were the one
I wanted my mistakes to be undone
But now I know it wasn't a mistake
I was being saved from undeniable heartache
What I was given was truly a gift
Making room for someone I was meant to be with
For reasons I will never understand
My heart made an unrelenting demand
To go find you and let you know
That I have never let my love for you go
And I'm glad I did because my love was real
And I wanted you to know just how I feel
That someone who shared my childhood years
Has a place in my heart and a part of my tears
I was always loyal and true

Never loved anyone the way I loved you
I have no regrets because love is a treasure
A wonderful feeling no lifetime can measure
I now walk away with love still inside
Praying that you let God be your guide
Find your true happiness and get back the real you
Don't ever give up whatever you do
I can tell you with confidence it's worth the fight
For I have now learned how to do it right
I've put you away in the corners of my mind
With a piece of my heart for you it's designed
Thank you so much for the revelation
The needed and priceless education
I truly appreciate what you've given to me
Thank you so much for setting me free

Day 3
Marc: There was a time that I needed you. Now I have learned to live without you. I already set you free.

Addison: I feel that I need to move on. Being connected to you is weighing me down. Even though the love I feel is real, it is not healthy.

The Power

You no longer have power over me
My peace of mind has set me free
I won't allow my love for you to
Take over me and make me blue
I wish that I could be like the people who
Hate you and think like they do
I had this idea that seemed it would work
Not knowing that you would act like a jerk
That we could be together and live happily
Live out our days reflectively
That we could stay married
Really be your wife
The one that was meant to be
in your life
We'd have a place
Simple and small
Being together
Most important of all
I'd finally have
Everything I need
You with me
Was all I'd ever need
I would drop everything
And run to you
Where I wanted to be
My whole life thru
I tried to make myself
As beautiful as I could
Wanted your approval
As anyone would
But I realized that
Shouldn't be
If you really loved me
You'd accept me for me
I wanted to be perfect
An enhancement for your arm

With grace and poise
And irresistible charm
But you mistreated me
What a brutal surprise
Devastated me
Could have caused my demise
A harsh cold blow
To a weakened heart
I wanted to love you
And you wanted no part
I imagined sitting with you
And touching your face
Listening to music
Just sharing your space
Sharing my thoughts with you
Love notes and devotions
Swaying each other
With love tempered motions
You kissing my hand
Tempting my mind
Caressing me softly
As you look in my eyes
kissing my shoulder
softly and sweetly
Fulfilling my heart
And soul so completely
dancing with me slowly
Our pulsating hearts touch
Enjoying the rhythm
Because I love you so much
Professing our love
That has lasted so long
Sweethearts since childhood
And still going strong
But that was a dream
Though sweet, unfulfilled

You broke down my hopes
Crushed my heart as you willed
It played in my head
As I thought it should be
But you treated me cold
Like you never loved me
So hard to accept
But I'm not the first one
With a broken heart
Since time has begun
My dream was to love you
Take care of your spirit
Wanted you to embrace love
And never fear it
To know that I've loved you
Since I was a girl
And now a grown woman
Still part of your world
Wake up to you everyday
Feeling joyful and complete
Facing any problems
Knowing we could defeat
But you defeated me
Your first true love
Hailed down on my head
Like storms from above
Demolished my dream home
And took my new name
The one that you gave me
In my life board game
Brought me back to reality
That this wasn't true
No longer together
No me and no you
But I will survive
My heart will go on

And any other redemptive
And broken heart song
I have to continue
And strengthen myself
Put the book of our love
Back up on the shelf
Because it is a fairytale
Too good to be true
Others have done it
But not me and you
Your love is no more
Must say my goodbyes
No matter how it hurts
It was all just lies
The memories were real
But that's all that is left
Must put them in boxes
Where keepsakes are kept
Too bad for us
We were a power force
Could have been dynamic
If we stayed the course
But I have to move on
Despite how I feel
Wish there was a magic word
To make my heart heal
I'll never stop loving you
Forever we'll be
The woman that cherished you
The man that loved me
Soon I'll learn to stop thinking of you
Every minute of every day
To let you go
I'll find a way
I don't want to erase you
Make you disappear

Like you never existed
Or weren't ever here
I must find a way
To soften the blow
Walk away
And let you go
It's hard to say goodbye
When your love is all I've known
And over the years it's grown and grown
Now to make it stop growing
Cut it off in it's path
Will not be fixed
With a warm bubble bath
Or nightly martinis
Or shopping sprees
This heartbreak has brought me
Down to my knees
I'll just have to start
With hour by hour
But I can no longer
Let you have the power

Day 4
Marc: All I ever wanted was to love you and take care of you. You never believed me. You couldn't see past your anger and hurt. I don't feel like you fought for us.

Addison: Marc, I don't need you to set me free. I always needed you to open up to me and tell me what you were feeling but it was so hard for you. There was a time when we were best friends and I miss that. I miss you. I miss the person that you were.

WHAT I MISS

I don't miss you, I miss who you were. The gentle and mild one is who I prefer. You said that you loved me and I believed because I felt it with each breath I released. You promised me everything and left me empty-handed. The way things turned out is not how we planned it, but life goes on, I'll cherish the memory and hold in my heart the love that's within me.

SPEAK

Speak to my heart
And not my mind
I am not the thinking kind
Not when it comes to love at least
I can not seem to tame that beast
It calls me out
It beckons me within
Takes me where I'm going
And sees where I've been
It tells me yes when I wanna say no
When I should stop it tells me to go
If it's love you speak of
Sing me a song
Write me a letter
Passionate and strong
I am a listener
Speak to me please
Will you put my troubled spirit
at ease?
You'll have my attention

Legs limp and weak
All you have to do
Is to my heart speak
Speak to it softly
Confident and slow
When it hears your voice
It will surely know
That you've come to play
Not for sport but for keeps
As you caress me with your words
And it jumps and leaps
The key to getting someone
To hear what you say
Is touching the heart
Slowly paving your way
To the reason for the action
The basis of belief
The catalyst for a warrior
The basement of grief
If you want one to understand
where you're coming from
You must speak to the heart
The resilient.. one
Make your point to the boss
The dreamer the hold
The one that can be heated
And warmed when it's cold
Intellect is crucial
And helps you succeed
But the heart can empower you
And make you bleed
The best thing you ever
Had in life
Your love, your husband
Your best friend, your wife
Were won with your heart

Betraying your mind
When it said I don't see it
The heart said, "your blind!"
If you really want something
Or love hard and strong
It doesn't matter if it makes sense
Is irrational or wrong
Your heart that's said
to be treacherous and cunning
Will lead you to love
And stop you from running
From what's unbelievably delightful
Wonderful and surreal
Convince you to be honest
And admit how you feel
I want to know it
What's deep inside
Come out dear heart
No longer hide
Its your innermost thoughts
And feelings I seek
But I'll never know them if you don't
Speak

Day 5
Marc: Sometimes I don't know what to say. You seem so strong & determined. I just back away.

Addison: It took both of us to fight. We need to be open and honest and show our true feelings. Sometimes we are afraid to show our hearts. That's why I believe they never healed.

THE BRAVE ONE

Don't be afraid
Be bold and empowered
Don't hide behind your exterior
Makes others feel inferior
But what is it really
Are you mean? Are you cruel?
Or are you just afraid of looking like a fool?
If everyone was afraid of that
We would never talk or laugh or chat
Some of the best things there are to do
To let down your guard and just be you
It doesn't come from self confidence
Dignity or poise
It comes from foolish pride
And limits your joys
Be brave and emboldened
Speak out don't hold back
Say what you feel just use insight and tact
Don't be afraid
Of what the response might be
The truth is invigorating and will set you free
From pinned up emotions
And deep down regrets
Your mind is a vacuum
And never forgets
So you'll carry it with you
The good and the bad
The bitter the sweet
The happy the sad

But letting it out
Will give you the power
To take on anything
Your enemies devour
Crescendo a roar
A yell or a shout
Do what you have to
To let it out
Don't be afraid
To show your heart
It's like sharing your knowledge
When you are smart
You show your brain
Everyday
Not caring what others think
Come what may
Will people say
Your heart is too massive
Temper it down
And be more passive
No because a big heart
Is pure
Lovable passionate
Straightforward and sure
It's confidence accountability
Willing to accept
That you're imperfect
And in some areas inept
It will make you a better person
Not afraid to take a leap
Realizing that the more you sow
The more you will reap
Be brave be strong
Don't hide behind pain
If you continue to hide
You've nothing to gain

Build up your courage
Be determined to live
For each and every moment
Your all to give
Don't be remembered
As selfish and afraid
Be the one with whom
Dreams are made
Reach out to people
You love and you know
Don't be afraid
Your emotions to show
Embrace the bad
And give it a hug
Say I welcome your teaching
And then give a shrug
Go where no one
Has dared to go
Be one with nature
Reflect the sun's glow
Mostly importantly
Love hard and real
Don't back down from fear
Or hesitate to feel
Tell someone you love them
No matter what the reply
Take all of your anxieties
And throw them to the sky
Be the brave one
The one that will
Never have to say
I lived my life the easy way

Day 6

Marc: One thing I've always loved about you, You speak your mind. Sometimes it gets on my nerves but I love you for it at the same time. When you left I was so angry. You knew I loved you and you left.

Addison: When you broke my heart the last time I just couldn't take it anymore. My heart can only take so much. I know that you loved me but that wasn't enough.

UNRELIABLE....trifling heart unrighteous, disposed, I stand here calm, serene and composed, feelings unuttered don't mean they're not true, just because they're rejected and shunned by you, unlovable life, rambled and confused, dismissive, unneeded, borrowed and used. Why didn't you fight for me, why didn't your love want us to be. Why didn't you beg to hold my hand? Why didn't my promise you demand? Wasn't I worth the passion and fight. Didn't I treat you good and right? Why did you let her take you away? Didn't you know that I would stay? If only you would have held my face, told me you love me and warmly embrace, I would have melted and burned from the heat, every obstacle we could have beat down and risen above, anything accomplished with our love. Instead you chose substitutes, bad impersonators, you can't refute. Hardened your shell and tightened your grip, took the longest miserable trip. Wrong and entitled to nothing I give, choosing an charm free life to live. What in the world were you thinking of, such a long hard fall from my sweet love. You had it all, what happened to you? Arrogant and mean, disrespectful you. Where did he come from this different man, was he always there, did I just not see, the person you were going to be. I thought that unconditional love and endurance would give our troubled love assurance but your youthful lust and boastful pride made it impossible to hide, the immature you that refused to grow even though I loved you so. I loved you so, my heart did beat for you, it pounded until I lost my breath and couldn't speak, made me weak and now the final truth I seek. Did you ever love me? Did you really care? Was I just an arm piece, a decoration a common ordinary relation. Was my love wasted on unreal, did you ever really feel what I felt for you inside?. My true feelings I will not hide. I am not ashamed for my heart was true, dedicated, faithful and loyal to you. I will soar knowing I was good, never sad, the best thing that you ever had. Without a doubt I say dear heart for as long as we have been apart I have lived loved and grown, my depth of love to others shown, never forgetting that you taught me how to survive thru pain even until now. You taught me heartache, longing aimlessly for your heart to be true and for you to see that I was all you ever needed, I was everything I could ever be but time has admitted that you couldn't contain it the blossoming flower named just for me. I wanted so for us to work but a higher power held back the wind. It stirred and said don't give yourself, on his heart you can't depend. He has been unfaithful every since you can recall, been dishonest, deceitful and wrong, if you go with him his heart will fail you and lead you to sadness for oh so long. Life has to teach him to value precious that what he had was one of a kind, someone that loved him thru and thru, a stronger love he will not find. He will be sentenced to struggle and cry from those that wish him ill, he'll come to see that he gave up on the one who always will, love him dearly, hold him in esteem and always eternally care, will want the best to touch his life been if you're not there. That usually comes along once in a lifetime but as a gift being given to you I sent someone deserving of your heart to be faithful loyal and true. Lessons learned and hardened exteriors result from deep heartache. Life will give so much and bless good work and some things from you take. Value all that you have endured for it has fortified, your strength, your faith, your lovesick heart and courage multiplied. Now your being is mature and nourished healthy, loving and viable. Be happy you didn't trust his heart because it is unreliable.

Day 7
Marc: I missed you so much that after a while I just became numb. I didn't think we

would ever get back together so I just learned to cope. That's all I was doing, coping not living ...and not really doing a good job of coping.

Addison: Marc, I had to leave. You've done and said some mean things to me. I've said some mean things too. It's not right and I apologize. Being hurtful doesn't accomplish anything but more hurt.

MADE

You made me
Afraid of the dark
You made me
Afraid to walk in the park
You made me
act the way I do
Strange & peculiar
Trusting only few
I blame you
For making me this way
I blame you
For my suffering everyday
I blame you
For everything wrong with me
Everything right
Is what I strive to be
You made me
reclusive and contrite
You made me
Lose my will to fight

Whoever knew that you could create
Something so amazingly
awkwardly great
You're my creator
My sculptor, my scientist in the making
I'm your Frankenstein
The human part I'm faking
Trying to transform
Into who I want to become
Difficult for many
Impossible for some
Blaming you for making me
Has stunted my transformation
I must now own
The responsibility for this creation
You drew me into your love
You taught my heart to break
But It was me who cherished you
And chose that risk to take
Love is a gamble, winner takes all
Loser goes home broke
No one breaks the fall
You made me discover
Who I am who I can be
But you are not to blame
Because I made me
Healing but not yet cured
Searching but not quite found
Broken but not into pieces
Grasping for air but haven't drowned
Making a new me
Has taken many many years
Sleepless worried nights
And millions and millions of tears
But when the job is done
Whenever that may be

I will be the one
Responsible for me

DESIRE OF THE HEART
I need healing
I need love
I need attention
I need understanding
I need time
I need laughter
I need caressing
I need touch
I need interaction
I need positivity
I need affection
I need belief
I need faith
I need guidance
I need praise
I need sunlight
I need rain
I need moonlight
I need sanity
I need today
I need tomorrow
I need forever
And ever
And ever after
I need together
I need apart
I need fulfillment
I need heart
I need fixing

I need mend
I need not to be broken
Again and again
Again
I need sleep
I need peace
I need yesterday
I need release
I need bonding
I need cheer
I need there
I need here
I need somewhere
I need sublime
I need yours
I need mine
I need us
I need we
I need shelter
I need thee
I need patience
I need them
I need strength
I need him
I need power
I need true
I need me
I need you

Day 8
Marc: I apologize for saying mean things too. Do you remember the day I asked you why don't you love me anymore? Why did

you stop loving me?

Addison: Learning to live without you has not been easy for me either. I know that you thought it was, but it was not. When I tried to talk to you, though you wouldn't sit down and talk with me and that hurt.

TIME & PLACE

I told him that I need a time and place
To meet sit down and talk
He took on a rocky trail
To argue, fuss and walk
Come with me
Go with me
Walk with me
He promised he'd tell me a place
Instead he took me nowhere
Said that he needed space
He wouldn't give me time
He only gave me never
I wanted to spend my life with him
Our love to last forever
He gave me a small area
A place to hang my head low
Every time I needed him to stay
He would always go
He finally gave me time
The time to weep and cry
Just enough hours to break my heart
and minutes to say goodbye
I told him I love roses

In return he gave me stems
I asked him to write me love songs
He wrote me funeral hymns
I wanted him to be faithful
He cheated on me instead
I asked for love and affection
And he kissed me on the head
I wanted him to hold me
But he patted me on the back
My favorite color is red
But he painted everything black
I wanted him to kiss me
But he pinched me on the cheek
I wanted him to talk to me
But he refused to speak
I wanted him to be honest
But instead he lied to me
I wanted to be bound to him
But he chose to set me free
I told him I was hungry
He refused to buy me food
I wanted to be treated politely
He insisted on being rude
I needed him to be my lifeline
To hold me close and tight
He watched me lose the battle
And wouldn't even help me fight
I needed his encouragement
All he did was criticize
I want him to put effort into us
But he never even tries
And when he talks to me he never looks into my eyes
Why?
He doesn't want me to see him
And what's inside his heart

I need to see the whole thing
But he'll only show me part
He wants to apologize to me
But he doesn't quite know how
He's waiting for the perfect time
But he needs to do it now
Before my heart grows cold toward him
And doesn't need him at all
He wants to carefully approach this love
And I just want to fall
I want him to be my sweetheart
My lover and my friend
I think this is the beginning
He thinks this is the end
He wants to hold onto it
But I want him to pass the ball
I need to talk to him everyday
But he will never call
I say his heart is broken
I know that it will mend
My heart is broken as well
I just don't pretend
He wants to be the victim
I want to be the healer
He likes to keep things secret
But I am a revealer
I like to see things truthfully
For what they really are
He likes to hide his wounds
I always show my scar
It seems that we are opposites
But we're very much the same
He thinks that our love has ended
And I'm the one to blame
He feels that our future is ruined
I know it's waiting there

I feel that we can both be fixed
Our hearts we can repair
We're broken battered and bruised
We're both weary and battle scarred
I managed to hit the ground softly
But he landed very hard
It broke him into pieces
And made him develop a shell
It just has to be cracked open
I know him very well
Inside he's soft and pliable
Able to bend and give
I want to dwell inside that place
But he just wants to live
Come with me
Go with me
Walk with me
Is what I call to his soul
You're only a fraction of what you should be
But I can make you whole
I'll give you a time and a place
Where we can bond and heal
You can't continue numb
You have to learn to feel
I'll give you what you need
Not the opposite to spite
You're in this battle by yourself
But I want to help you fight
You've been giving me the opposite
Of what I really need
And if you continue hurting me
I will surely bleed
Just hold my hand and walk with me
This is a different time and place
You have to stop turning your back on me
And let me see your face

Give me roses not stems and thorns
Walk with me in the park
Shed your light on your true inner self
Don't keep me in the dark
Write me the song you promised
So many years ago
Don't wait for the perfect time to come
Because It will never show
Time waits for no one
The place is here an now
Tell hostility it's performance has ended
Leave the stage after taking it's bow
Replace the stage with your kindness
The audience with my smile
Take your time don't rush things
Just stay here for a while
Hearts can't be mended overnight
Wounds can't be cared for and healed
If we don't find a place and time
To have them all revealed
Walk me down the path love
Come with me sweetheart
Give me a time and a place
And I'll give you my heart

Day 9
Marc: I didn't want to talk to you. I can admit it now. I was afraid. I have missed you. I didn't know how to deal with it. I've been broken. I've been troubled. I felt betrayed , hurt and alone.

Addison: Dear Marc, I never stopped loving you. I could never stop loving you. I just couldn't take the hurt anymore. I did grow cold toward you for a while but it has never been my intent to hurt you. I have prayed for you every night, that you have peace in your heart and that you are safe.

MY PRAYER, "GIVE MY SOUL REST"

I go to sleep every night
Feeling broken hearted
Sometimes crying
I fantasize
I dream of you
I wake up
And thoughts of you are still there
I check my mail
And my phone messages
I try not to long for your call
But to no avail
I have to wait
I don't expect anymore
That ended long ago
I just pray for the day
That I don't long
I just wait
Then maybe I can go from waiting
To hoping
From hoping
To maybe one day
From maybe one day
To maybe never
From maybe never
To it would be a nice surprise
From it would be a nice surprise

To reality
Whatever that may be
Just let it be
And please let him be blessed
And give my soul peace
And rest

Day 10
Marc: Dear Addison, You pray for me? I pray for you. I never want harm to come to you. I always wanted us to be okay. I always knew we were meant for each other. You were perfect for me and you always loved me for me. I will always love you for that.

Addison: Dear Marc, I understood how you felt because I felt the same. I felt betrayed and alone too. I didn't want to think about it anymore but in the back of my mind, you were always there, always present.

THE HOPE
The hope of you keeps me strong
Keeps me holding on
What is going on
This is where you belong
In my arms
Safe and warm
Here and now
Let's make a vow
We can learn how

To coexist
Form a mighty fist
To fight off the negative
Punch it in the face
Take it out at the knees
Hear me please
Where are you
I need you
Tell me you
Love me still
Love you I will
I cherish you
I cherish us
And everything we represent
Don't know where our love went
Too much time spent
Being apart
I miss your heart
I need your heart
Please give me your heart
Let's make a new start
What's going on inside
I hope you will confide
In me, I am your friend
I have always been
Please let me in
What's going on with you?
What can I do?
Let me feel you
Stop hiding from me
Please set me free
If you talk to me
I'll understand
I'll take your hand
I've extended mine
Everything will be fine

I love you so much
I want to feel your touch
Tell me what it is
We can have each other
It doesn't make a difference
Everything is different
Here and now
Today is the day
I need to hear you say
You love me, that's all
The hope of hearing you say those words
Keeps me going, keeps me strong
And at the same time breaks me down
Hurts my soul
Please make me whole
And say you love me
No one has to know
It's between you and I
just tell me so
An then you can go
Walk away from me
I'll set you free
Just say that you still love me
I know you still love me
I can continue living with those words in my heart
They will feed it and sustain it
Then I can contain it
Then I can cope
With only the hope

Day 11
Marc: Dear Addison, I still love you very

much. I still care. I don't want you to go anywhere. I hide my feelings & keep them inside hoping they will go away. I know I have done wrong but I can't change it. But I do apologize for breaking your heart; The one that always loved me.

Addison : Marc, We were meant for each other. I have always believed that. The fact that I have loved you for who you are, not what you do or what you have is what has sustained that love and made it unmovable. Even throughout the problems, I always felt your true feelings for me. I just wanted you to understand that true love is not just words or even just feelings it is everything you do, everything you say, everything you are.

THE STORY OF US
First let me say
This Is a special day
Winter Fall Summer or Spring
Flowers bloom and birds sing
Love is in the air everywhere
Look around you'll see it there
If you don't you'll feel it
Just feel it
My imagination full of hope
Here we are
What's there for us?
Love just love
External love
Eternal love

Everlasting love
It won't go away
And I want it to stay
I want it to be
The essence of me
I put it on
It fits my form
It keeps me mellow
And soft and warm
This love
My love
Let me tell you about my love
This love letter
Serves as a memory
Of what is real
Surreal
I feel
It's the best thing I ever had
Why?
It has caused me to fly
Not always good
But the essence of goodness
Not always soft
But the essence of softness
Always promising and hopeful
Forever emotional
So emotional
My heart is full
Why?
I love him so?
Why?
I don't know
Why does it grow?
Where does it come from?
The birth of our love
Steady and easy

Painless with no complications
No anesthesia the full effect
In surround sound
Burst into the world
Ready to go
Do you know what you're doing?
No
Do you know what your feeling?
No
I just know I love him so
Why?
I don't know
Cute and tall
Dark and handsome
Eyes glow
Emotions flow
I don't know where it's coming from
Made for you
Made for me
We just know
In love we grow
Possessive Attracted
Immature Treacherous
What are the rules?
We're a bunch of fools
Headed for heartbreak
Why does my heart ache?
What is this feeling
That I'm feeling?
Emotions reeling
Where did you go?
I don't know
I'll let you go
But please
Don't forget about me
Don't forget about me

Day 12
Marc: I am planning a date for us. Will you go with me? As soon as you read this let me know or if you need time to think about it, I understand.

Addison: Dear Marc, Your apology means a lot to me. Thank you. I broke the rules. I opened your message for today. Yes I will go on a date with you.

GRACIOUS

I'm grateful for the opportunity
To dance with you tonight
Your hand on the small of my back
We sway to the beat Under the stars
Their light beaming down on me
It's hard to imagine that moments like this
Are absolutely free
I'm grateful for the privilege
To sit and talk with you
Reminisce about the past
Sometimes reinventing, "Is that the way it happened?
I don't know, who cares"
I just know you were there, taking steps with me
Walking thru life carefree, let's be that again

If only for a few minutes, a few hours
I'm grateful for my hands that glide across
yours shoulder blades
Like playing a piano, like the leaves in fall
Feeling that place behind your ribs, take
your spot in that small
Corner where your name is indelibly etched
Feel it beat for you and sway under the stars
I'm grateful that I'm alive to see your face if
only once more
So beautifully aged like no time has gone by
with life
Under our belts wisdom is all we've gained,
we're still the same
Just older, more experienced, now we know
what life is about
Though still trying to get it right, so grateful
to see you tonight
Take my hand or kiss my cheek , hug me
tightly like you'll never
See me again before you leave. We don't
know what tomorrow brings
I'm grateful for right now, today, just sway
As we dance the night away

Day 13
Marc: Dancing with you last night was wonderful. I haven't held you close like that for so long. I guess these letters were a good idea. I apologize for not being nice in the beginning. I was angry. Please let me know how you feel about these letters.

Addison: I love these letters. You know I've always loved letters. I wish you would write me one everyday. I still remember you promised to write me a song or a love poem but you never did. I still think about that. I've always wanted a love letter from you.

Marc: Addison, I remember that promise and I wrote it. I just never gave it to you because I didn't think you would like it. I've kept it for all of these years. I will send it to you.

THE WAY
The way I walk you to class
The way you kiss me goodbye
The way you call me on the phone
The way you don't want to say goodbye
The way you put your hand in mine
The way you promise you will always love me
The way you get jealous when I talk to someone else
The way you feel safe with me
The way you feel when I hold you close and hug you tight
The way you feel in my arms close to my heart
The way you brag that I am smart & strong
The way you believe in me
The way you are there for me when I need you most

The way you have my back when things get tough
The way you want to save yourself until we get married
The way your hand feels caressing my cheek
The way you say you want to spend forever with me
The way you look pleadingly when I am upset with you
The way you love me more than anybody else
The way you beg for forgiveness when you hurt my feelings
The way you make my body feel when you are close to me
The way you make my heart feel even when we're far apart
The way you consume my thoughts when we are not together
The way no one could ever take your place
The way I long for you all of the time
The way I know you will always love me
The way I know I will always love you

Addison: The Way
The way you walked me to class
The way you kissed me goodbye
The way you called me on the phone
The way you never wanted to say goodbye
The way you would reach your hand back for me
The way you promised you would always love me
The way you would get jealous when I talked to someone else
The way you made me feel safe

The way you would hold me close & tight & open your jacket for me to come in when I was cold & the way I felt in your arms close to your heart
The way you bragged that I was smart
The way you always believed in me
The way you were there when I needed you most
The way you had my back when things got tough
The way you wanted me to save myself until we got married
The way your hand felt caressing my cheek
The way you wanted to spend forever with me
The way you would look pleadingly when I was upset with you & tug at your hat when you were nervous
The way you loved me more than anyone else
The way you begged for forgiveness when you hurt my feelings
The way you made my body feel when you held me close
The way you made my heart feel even when we were apart
The way you consumed my thoughts when we were not together
The way no one could ever take your place
The way I longed for you all of the time
The way I knew that you would always love me
The way that I knew that I would always love you

Day 14

Marc: Addison, lets go to the park. We will take a walk and talk. I'm coming to pick you up. Is that okay?

Addison: Yes, I'll be waiting. :-)

RIDING IN YOUR CAR

I want to ride with you in your car
Simply because it's where you are
I see you pass by everyday
And hope that you will look my way
I wish I didn't have to pretend
That you and I are on the mend
I wish that you would look at me
And where I am, you want to be
I want the chance to look at you
Not thru glass but virtual and true
Have conversation, sip coffee or tea
Reminisce about you and me
Work on our relationship
Take a romantic weekend trip
Start back up where we left off
Make it better warm and soft
Make it hot steamy and sweet
Be brave adventurous and not retreat
Take our love forward and don't look back
Get our relationship back on track
Let's make it work, let's figure it out
Discover what this love is all about
Let's act like teenagers with innocence
Like star-crossed lovers without any sense

Let's ride around and play music loud
Dance and sing, no seriousness allowed
Get reacquainted and remember how
We fell in love and if we can now
Be that couple we used to be
Deep in love, inseparable and free
Free to take each others heart
And care for it and never part
Love each other unconditionally
Respect, appreciation unfailingly
Growing older together, happy and content
Regarding each other as heaven sent
Going around our town, our love exhibition
Our future and plans in position
I love the idea of us coming together
Promising to separate again, never
Let's go take a ride together in your car
Because I want to be where you are

Day 15
Marc: Addison, our day was wonderful. You are so beautiful. You are the love of my life. I should have fought harder for us but I promise I will from now on.

Addison: Marc, Our picnic was wonderful. It reminded me of the things we used to do together. We both should have fought harder. I will fight harder too.

REACH
I dreamed that you came for me,
put out your hand and reached for me
You told me you would always come for me
Open your heart and let me see
How you feel and who you are, who you want to be
Close my eyes and open my mind, and truly set me free
Comfortable feelings, awesome, appealing
Amazing revelation about our situation
We find ourselves in, for now is not then
Yesterday is gone, tomorrow is a dream
No matter how hopeless it may seem
Love will save it, make it survive
As long as we remain alive
The heart connects no matter how far
When you look in the sky and see a star
Think of me for I am thinking of you
Because I know you love me too
I am willing to learn what this lesson will teach
Just know that I am within your reach

Day 16

Marc: Dear Addison, I am reaching for you.

Addison: Dear Marc, I am taking your hand.

HOLDING HANDS

Saying what you see is what you get
And you ain't seen nothing yet
You say the jokers win and the deuce is wild
Well beg of pardon from this flower child
Holding your hand in intimate hour
Holds such passionate loving power
Like praying mantis stance and prayerful pose
Like the sweet gentle smell of a blossomed rose
Everything seen is not as it's felt
Your touch is one of a kind
If someone sees me holding your hand
The vision can't explain to the mind
That your palm is like a secret potion
Your fingers like intricate bends
Grasping my warmth and encompassing the feel
And hoping it never ends
For it's like feeling life flowing
Where warmth and security are kept
Like ripples on water and breezes
So fulfilling and precious she wept
For him it is blanketing coldness
Roaring heat from his soft fingertips
Feeling her heartbeat gently pounding
As he clings to the girth of her hips
Sweet love hold my hand don't let it go
It's my shield from apprehension and strife
Just the pull and the sway of your hand
Assures me that I'm needed in your life
As we are walking and your strides become double to mine
I fall behind and slow down the pace

Then you hold out your hand and reach back for me
And I see the love in your face
It's the grasp that let's me know
That you won't let me fall
That you will never let it go
Or let me get hurt at all
The grip may weaken as we grow older
But this for sure I know
Our love will never diminish
It can only grow
The lines on the surface of your strength filled hands
Are a path to your heart and mine
The veins of your wrist taut and risen
Flow the blood of your soul divine
We belong to each other in a bonded mosaic
As intricate as our fingers intertwine
We knew from the beginning it would never end
Forever yours, you forever mine

Day 17
Marc: Dear Addy, I love you and I want you back in my life. This time I want to do it right. We have a second chance and I am grateful. When we were apart it was like a piece of me was missing. I promise that I am committed to making this work. Those promises I made so long ago still mean something to me and I want a chance to keep them.

Addison: Dear Marc, I love you. we are blessed to have a second chance. I am willing to try again, this time even harder. I think that if we forgive and put the past behind nothing will get in our way.

LOVE STORY

It's like you're having a love affair
In a way I'm having one too
Your proclivity is loving me
And mine is loving you
It took me a long time to understand
Love can come in any form
It can be simple
It can be complex
Can be cold can be soft and warm
It's the way we were made
To embrace all that comes
For good and even for bad
From the worst thing that ever happened to me
To the best thing I ever had
Before I was hurt and couldn't understand
What this life had in store for me
All the twists and turns and disappointments
And the pain that wouldn't let me be
I couldn't reconcile I couldn't comprehend
why love would allow me to.....
Love you so deeply so strong and so hard
But never give me to you
To come so close and be so far
Is a pain that can't be described

It cuts so deep and bleeds so long
And the scar you're unable to hide
You bandage it up and cope with the hurt
And believe it will get better in time
Convincing yourself that it's not real
That it's really just all in your mind
I've seen how you've chosen to cope with the pain
You too pretend it's not there
You rid yourself of all that reminds you
Of me and our love affair
You choose to ignore me and feelings within
And act as if love passed you by
When truly you had all the love in the world
From someone that was willing to try
From someone that was willing to give up her life
For yours and all you desire
Would walk to the edge of the world and back
Just so you could soar even higher
That would give her own life if it meant that you
Could be at peace in your heart
And have everything that you ever wanted
And forgive me for us being apart
If that's not real to you and you don't believe
Then you'll never truly know love's essence
For everything that I have lost in my life
It was worth it to be in your presence
You see I've never once doubted your worth or your value
From the first time I saw your face
I knew you were special and meant for me
And no one could take your place
It was written in time

It was in the plan it was always meant to be
For us to experience what love really means
From the depths that only rival the sea
Have you ever watched the sea at night
And followed the crashing waves flow
And wonder how it's possible for the depths
To descend as far and deep as they go
To experience true love at it's deepest core
Is like knowing all there is to be learned
Its like figuring out the most complex puzzle
But still for more knowledge you yearn
If true love was easy and only soft
Not hard and crude and complex
Then we would think it was purely physical
About wanting and pleasure and sex
That all we had to do was give and
Then we would surely receive
Anything we want and desire to have
We only just have to believe
But that's not the way that true love works
It's spiritual wholesome and pure
It does not hold grudges it does not divide
Does not give up but endures
It is kind and loyal not selfish or haughty
Not puffed up angry or jealous
It's everything good rebukes everything bad
And if practiced it will never fail us
Sometimes we are meant to experience the bad
Not only to appreciate the good
But to learn just what the good really means
What it is, when it is, why it should
Where it is, how it is, why it is, that it is
How do we become it's partakers
How can we be a part of what's real and true
And separate us from the fakers

From those who claim that they love what is good
But rejoice in what is bad
And say they want to make us happy
But laugh secretly when we are sad
I want us to be a part of something sincere
Let our struggle not be in vain
Let all the lessons learned guide us thru
Let us receive all there is to be gained
Let us continue to learn what love really is
And teach each other and those we know
Those we cherish lets bring them in
To embrace us and help our love grow
Grow into what it always was
And forever was meant to be
To help them understand our love
The story of you and me
And may their experiences with love and pain
Help them to understand
That I was always meant to be your love
And you to be my Man
That you were my everything and I was yours
And we will never give up the fight
To be together eternally
And get this love thing right
To know inevitably we will be together
Either here or on the other side
The other side of living that is
Let the Creator be our guide
You see hurt and anger has chosen to set me free
I can no longer bear
The depth of anguish to which it has taken me

I wasn't meant to be there
It's duty has been to make me aware
And for me to learn what to do
But when the time comes it will let me go
For it knows I belong to you
The love to be made will be wholesome, just
Without guilt or fear of wrong
It will be the completion as well as the beginning
Of our life long composed heart song
Worth the wait and approved by love
Endless timeless surreal
Every dream desire and longing
All the love that we can feel
All the love our hearts can take
And just when we thinks it's done
The love will start all over again
As our bcing and breath become one
As our lives intertwine so intricate and deep
And we all dwell together in bliss
In peace and calm and happiness too many pleasures to list
The pain that got us here forgotten
But the knowledge kept and embraced
The love accomplished and understood
No broken heart pieces not even a trace
This love story is one of many but to us
It's the only one
It seems that it started years ago
But it's only just begun
It hurts to learn but it's worth the pain
Our love was meant to be
You can fight it if you want
But you're wasting your energy
Instead won't you try to embrace this gift
Unwrap it slowly take a deep breath, close

your eyes
Imagine us, imagine us, with no more goodbyes

Day 18
Marc: I love you, Addy
Addison: I love you too, Marc
Marc: Soon it will be our last love note day.
Addison: I know. I'm gonna miss them.
Marc: I don't think it should be the last
Addison: I don't either

Day 19
Marc: Tomorrow is the first day. Are you ready?
Addison: Yes, I am ready.
Marc: I am ready too.

Day 20
Marc: I'll be there in a little while to pick you up.
Addison: I'll be waiting.

    When Marc and Addison went back to the mediator, They told her about the twenty day love notes, informing her that they weren't really love notes at first, but they soon began really listening and understanding what the other was saying and then responding to one another. They told her that they now understood the reason behind the letters and confessed that they eventually broke the rule of waiting to read the notes. When she asked them what was the most important thing they learned. They replied that they would never stop writing love letters and to always live, feel, become and say those Three words, "I love you".

~~~~~~~~~~~~~~

~PEACE OF ME~

The human heart always has hope, even if it is just the tiniest glimmer and it will continue to hope until there is no inkling of a spark. If there is one little spark, hope will hang on.

FACES
…remind you of places you've been before.
Eyes remind you why you need much more.
Lips give motion to words unspoken.
Ears to hear sweet music when your heart is broken. Noses smell the perfume that reminds you of me.
My face reminds you of who I used to be.
Who I am now can be found in my heart, my most important body part.
There are those that think they know me
There are some that really do
There are few who feel my intention
And what I'm trying to do
Unguarded, open and grateful

For everything I receive
Vulnerable, frail and gracious
And willing to believe
That things will gradually become better
As long as I continue grow
And be the kind of person
That you would like to know
My hand is lovingly extended
Outreached for warm embraces
Emanated from inside
And reflected on your faces

SHINE
A sea of a million faces, each one with a story engraved
Some with heroic nature, some with the need to be saved
A cloud of unforgiving and anxious hangs over and threatens to shower
To drown aspirations in terror and snatch away hope's power
Oh Where is compassion's umbrella? Is there someone to hold it still?
Drenched in my own insecurities, I quietly say "I will"
Emboldened by love and desire to encourage inspire and embrace
Taken over by love's good nature, light of truth beams brightly from my face
Hold onto my hand thru my voice , hear it whisper with roses and pain
Relating my past experiences; from sharing I can not refrain

I bathe in the sun of your praises, your love, admiration and gifts
You make me soar much higher build my confidence and my countenance lifts
Raise your hand if you feel my emotion, say I do if you rock with my flow
See there is so much gained from your reaction than you could ever possibly know
My mind is filled with the knowledge that more learning is what I demand
While my heart is filled with gratitude for everything be it minor or grand
My hands shake with nerves and pure energy, my back has withstood hard knock life
As I gaze at your emanated glowing I'm relieved of all trouble and strife
See my trouble heart has given me problems, that's what I call it , my problem child
Couldn't behave if my life depended on it which and it does so I'll be calm and mild
I'm in love with love of my family, my friends, my enemies my foes
What I deal with in turmoil and struggle has sent me places that no one else knows
The passion I feel when I dream when I think when I speak when I write
Takes over my being and symmetry as I pour onto paper at night
As we walk around greeting each other and engage in light conversation
What's deeper is not brought to the surface, withholding inner self information
As you see I'm an open book, at times I admit to a fault

It's like living in front of a mirror that reflects everything that I'm taught
See I know that a lesson learned is valuable, no matter how painful the ride
Because within those layers of self and existence your integrity and character are tried
I want you to say of me; when I'm no longer here or deceased
That her words taught me the power of pain, that anxieties must be released
That wearing your heart on your sleeve can be problematic and hurtful at times
But she let go of it all with her poetry her stories and truth - ridden rhymes
That she empowered those weak with her abilities, with her lyrics soothed the aching of their heart
That she was not afraid to say what she was thinking or her triumphs and failures impart
That's all I could ever ask for, that's all I ever will need
I feel with a fires intensity when someone else hurts I bleed
Please receive what give in the best way, it always has the best of intention
So many people & things that I'm grateful for far too many to mention
But know this that I'm filled with love, so much so that I've overcome
My fear of performance art & showing myself to some
There are vast amounts of persons with their skill & words they give
By the vow to humanity their lead, by it's credence they are determined to live

I join them in the movement, I believe in words that heal
I believe that you can help someone, if you humbly & honestly reveal
I'm aware that the world has heard many voices but they have yet to be empowered by mine, so I will let go of my apprehensions and let it shine, let it shine

SEASONS

I share with you my truth
These feelings from my youth
I am an open book
For anyone to look
I share because its noble
Its mannered and polite
The purpose is to visualize
My demeanor being contrite
Rewind your past to childhood
The stories many and vast
Delightful smells and sounds
Brighten a dark and troubled past
So many people are everywhere
Yet no one has a clue
The sad and gloomy secrets
That have defined this thing called you
Innocence exploring nature
While trouble is throwing rocks
Running thru the hallways
And sliding on your socks
Smelling breakfast cooking

Running to catch the bus
Scanning the sea of faces
For someone you can trust
Walls closing in around you
Kneeling to hide your face
No one hears your cries for help
In this scary lonesome place
Running to mommy and daddy
Stealing their warmness to sooth your cold
Feeling the heartbeat of someone who loves you
Travels with you until you grow old
A ray of hope some sunlight
A distant voice of reason
Like a silvery shiny nickel
Or the changing of the season
Fall is the always the favored
Welcoming autumn breeze
Crisp and cleansing winds
Gently rock my soul at ease
Leaves floating and changing colors
Where are you going? Come dance with me
Is there something that you're running from
As you escape that massive tree?
Costume changes so many times
As if parading at a ball
Twirling around in their tattered skirts
forming mountains as they fall
Come slowly the graying winter
Your procession commands attention
Wrapped in blanket like clothing
We mourn the sun's dissention
Looking up at bluish-gray and
Scattered white cotton pillows
Spreading thin, then bunching up
Into endless fluffy billows

Holding your boyfriend's hand
Resting your head on his chest
Being silly with your best friend
While studying for a test
Oh heroic snow we beg you
Kill the villainous school day
Let us celebrate the victory
While we run outside and play
Our noses red and freezing
Our fingers cold as ice
Watch out for lurking shadows
Pretending to be nice
Sunshine melt the sickle heart
Of the slithering childhood thief
Bring bathing salts with April showers
Caress and soak the invisible grief
Come spring jumping into action
Causing butterfly fluttering hearts
No antidote for the fever
That its whimsical presence starts
Concentration almost impossible
The warmth producing rays
Force garments to shed their owners
On seemingly endless days
Parks full of baby carriages and lovebirds
Holding hands yet bashful and coy
Young love sprouting with the flowers
Blissful weddings resounding with joy
As the heat intensely rises
Runners perspiring panting for breath
Summer announces it's early arrival
From the earth's twirling universal depth
Anxiously awaiting the finale
An echoing round of applause
A roaring standing ovation
Bowing gracefully while hiding your claws

Howling and whistling for the performance
And the school days' curtain call
Don't forget me for I shall return soon
The next act will premier next Fall

WEEPING WILLOW

I stare out of the window at THE BIG OAK TREE
it seems that it is staring back at me
The corners of my mind making even fold
Edge to edge as the stories told
Over and over systematically
Then all of a sudden sporadically
Bury my head in the softness of a pillow
Wishing that tree was a weeping willow
Then it could wail and cry for me
Why won't these feelings let me be
Blowing in the wind running in a field
The walls of this house a protective shield
Growing pains and confusing thought
Respectful manners are what you're taught
But there are no lessons for adolescence
Natural exuberance and effervescence
Youthful trust and naiveté
Threaten your innocence everyday
Playing with dolls and giggling fun
Never fearing anyone
No one really ever knows
Who are enemies who are foes
They walk around mixed up with the good
Pretending to be what they know they should
But secrets and lies define their heart

Viciously tearing lives apart
Pray for those not knowing what to do
For it could have easily been you
For those who have escaped the pain
Whose mind and inner calm remain
Cry for those who fight to live
Reach your hand and comfort give
Wrap your figurative arms around
The injured soul and sorrow sound
Private sufferings emotional blues
Dark indigo and shadowed hues
Saddened countenance pretense face
Blissful outbursts in their place
Sacred relationship with honored being
On bended knee when no one is seeing
Talking to the invisible friend
Helping your broken parts to mend
Quiet whispers slight melody
Humming a tune composed for thee
Harmony envelops and cradles me
As I sit there staring at the giant tree

THE ANSWER pt. 2
I'm free I'm free no one is bothering me
Nothing to run from
Nothing to explain
No logical reason for why
I'm going insane
Fear in my pocket
Trouble in my hand
Lost in the memories
I don't understand
Filled with compassion
Emptied of hate

A crevice of love
It begins to create
There is always a question
That eats away like cancer
But no matter the cost
Love is always the answer

THE WAY…TO LOVE

The Way to love
Is with your heart
It's the only body part
To give to one
You desire most
The one you want to
Hold you close
Hold them close
To your heart
To hear it pounding
To make it start
A pitter patter
Love tap tap
Places uncharted
off the map
Make it beat
Make it play
You're supposed
To love that way
It's not the face
Not the hair
Not the things
That make you stare

It's the things that make
It skip a beat
A champion love
You can't defeat
It never leaves
Just changes lanes
And takes a route
May cause you pains
But can come back
To find the way
To find love lost
A brighter day
Light the path
Blaze the trail
Build a love that
Can not fail
Rev it up
Quicken the pace
Pick up the beat
Run in place
Catch your breath
Slow it down
Get the rhythm
Make it pound
That's the heat
You want to make
Physical contact
Is sometimes fake
Steal the heart
Work it out
It's what true love
Is all about
Shock the system
Yell "it's clear"
the way it feels
When they are near

Most importantly
Take your time
Pace yourself
Slowly climb
The mountain of love
That works you out
Become a believer
Get rid of doubt
And don't give up
If not returned
It takes time
To feel the burn
If love is lost
Patiently wait
For a heart transplant
To set it straight
Steady moving
Never stop
Keep your pace
Until you drop
Into their arms
And let them feel
Your quickened heartbeat
That won't keep still
Its the heart that's key
To love that's real
If it gets broken
It will heal
It's the only way that's worthy of
Your precious heart
The way...to love

EULOGY PT. 2

".....if you don't understand why I grieve for you, you don't know how true love feels. Everything inside of me my heart always reveals. My grief is for the loss of you, the loss of what we had. Every time I think of us it makes me feel so sad. What hurts the most is that you never loved me, at least not the way I loved you. So grieve the past, move on with life is what I have to do.

SOLACE PT. 2 (THE SEA)

I woke up this morning to a beautiful sight
The waves were crashing and the sun was bright
Mind boggling hues spread like eagles flying
Dolphins jumping and seagulls crying
Lost in the quiet noise of the sea
Nothing weighing heavily or bothering me
Secrets of life held deeply in my heart
I gave to the wind, let it transcend into art
Rolled with the tide, bounced off the rays
Floated thru the air getting lost in the days
Oh such glory, where the water meets the sky
Appreciation and honor for this amazement have I

GONE

It is gone, never to return; oh how I wish my heart did not yearn

it has incinerated into ashes and dust, pry
my fingers and let go I must
Will you take care of me rain and sun?
Promise you will; for you're the only one
That knows my pain, my inside destruction;
help me to rebuild a solid construction
One that is whole, one that won't break, one
that is immune to any heartache
I want to be free, can't keep holding on. I
just want this hurt to be gone

THE VISITOR

Come to see me sadness, come visit my
despair
I welcome your arrival please pull up a chair
I know you won't stay long, your visit will
be brief
Comfort will come after you and bring me
some relief
My heart is aching desperately, it feels like I
will die
But I know that if I just hold on and let time
pass me by
The wounds will finally heal, the soreness in
my chest
Will slowly but surely dissipate and put my
pain to rest
So sit down and stay a while but don't think
that you will stay
You can cover me with gloom but then you
must go away

POSSIBILITIES

If you would just believe you could see another possibility
If you can forgive anything is possible
Open your heart and mind and find that everything will be okay, the next time you see the light of day
Say a prayer of thanksgiving and make a promise to love
love when it is not easy, love when it is the most difficult task, no one should have to ask, because this is a command, no one can demand but a request for your best is a gift to you. Forgiveness heals your heart and supplies your mind with the freedom to be every possibility you can not see

POSSIBILITIES PT. 2

It is probable that you can be unstoppable if you can live and learn to forgive, nothing you do will elude you and you have the propensity to see any possibility because when forgiveness is in your heart your healing can start and everything that you know, everything you thought you knew will blossom in to love and blessings from above. When your goals and plans you rearrange, your life will change and it might seem strange but forgiveness is for yourself, your emotional health so before you love gift and someone's spirits try to lift, spend time with you because you can not give what you do not have, what you do not own. Spend time alone and good habits hone your skills as a giver a good life-liver and right here and now make this vow, this promise to self to not put love on the shelf, take it down and pass it around. Believe it, receive it and you will achieve it, anything that you want will be yours, all open doors and then you will have the power, defeat to devour and hold it open for your friend, your relationships mend.

Anything is within your reach, if you are willing to be taught, then and only then will you be capable of teaching and another soul reaching because you now have within, the tools to begin. So be determined and open, set yourself free to these heartfelt pleas and you will develop with ease your capabilities and walk in the light of your possibilities

FRIEND Pt. 2

My friend my prayer for you today
Is that you give and receive along the way
Love and be loved, hold and behold
Embrace the warmth and come in from the cold
Live and let live, go and let go
Let bygones be bygones and accept and bestow
Hold on to your memories but let go of the pain
From animosity and vengeance learn to refrain
Forgive and forget, accord and beseech
May all of your dreams be within your reach

IGNORE RANT

I'm tired of being ignored, I'm tired of feeling alone
I'm tired of being the caring one and being on my own
Always on a limb, extending the loving hand
Why some don't reach out me, I do not understand
I am not needy or desperate but I am troubled and wanting
The difference is love in my heart with a task that's arduous and daunting
I'm complete within myself, I have family and love requited
Into my circle of life so many I have invited
I want to embrace the power of loyalty and being kind
Not forgetting where you came from, freeing and expanding your mind
Small actions like sending a card, making a phone call and saying hello
Is that too much to ask for? It's the only way I know
I believe in holding hands, sharing words and giving hugs
I'm discouraged by apathy and selfishness and seemingly virtual shrugs
A text, an email, a message; there are so many ways
To reach out to someone you care for; to brighten up their days
But I will never stop. My way is best to me
I will always let love be my answer; that's

how it's going to be

"TO THOSE WHO HAVE TURNED THEIR BACKS ON ME & DON'T CARE ENOUGH TO TURN AROUND"
To those who have turned their backs on me and don't care to turn around
Keep walking, keep on walking, I will not make a sound
I will not call your name, I will not shed a tear
If you don't want to be my friend, I do not want you here
Your back is so beautiful, it's all I want to see,
As you show the person you truly are and walk away from me
I hope you never need me, I hope that there is someone you have
Someone you can depend on, who's back you have not stabbed
Because if you ever call or reach for me I'm gone
I will no longer stay here for you to trample on
What you don't know is my beauty, for there are no eyes behind your head
No vision for you to notice even if I was dead
You never took the time to get to know my eyes
If I was standing in front of you, you would

realize
That to have me on your side is an advantage present and clear
A companion for better or worse, an ally always near
But you chose to walk away, so as I watch you fade away
I will not regret, but I will never forget and I will not beg you to stay
I learned long ago that anyone that's worth your time
Will withstand any troubled winds, will any mountain climb
Will swim across the ocean, will brave a desert storm
Will give you the clothes right off their backs just to keep you warm
I would have given you anything, I would have sacrificed
Whatever it took to stand by you, I would have paid the price
But one of the best lessons I've learned and I hold onto it's girth
Is that the way that someone treats you is what they feel you're worth
So since I'm nothing to you and respect for me you lack
So long, goodbye for the last time because you can not come back

DOUBLE HEART
Double heart, trouble heart

Broken and confused
Feeling sad and lonely
Sorrowful and used
Why do you have two faces
How do you sleep at night
Knowing that you are deceptive
and don't treat people right
Always in pieces and crumbled
Like paper on the floor
Not finished with yesterday's problems
Yet continue to open the door
To the next hardship and struggle
When there is no time to heal
How does it work when you are doubled
Can you really feel?
Or do you just go around starting fires
That you can not put out
Making people angry,
Causing them to scream and shout
Please stop me from letting love in
When I can not handle it
You are becoming weak and tired
You need to rest a bit
Please try to become just one
Two is way too much
I feel every whisper of emotion
I hear every loving touch
Confusion does not become me
It makes me look insane
If you give me a minor respite
I promise I will not complain
Make up your mind and tell me
What to do and where to go
Because as long as you are double
I will never know

THE WOMAN

Hello how are you?
Have I met you before
I recognized your face
As you walked thru the door
There is something about your smile
That seems vaguely familiar
your movement though graceful
Is somewhat peculiar
You remind me of a girl
I met long ago
That was carefree and giddy
Face lit with life's glow
Her body was thin
And her symmetry quite simple
A pretty round face
Adorned with a dimple
And your voice reminds me
Of her rhythm and charm
Inviting and warm
With no cause for alarm
Calm and collected
Cool and laid back
Respectful to others
With etiquette and tact
But the thing about you
that is different
from her
Is your hips are much fuller
which is what I prefer
Your legs are larger
Carry ample behind
Your eyes are inviting
endearing and kind

The girl that I knew
was beautiful like you
But not as much confidence
Though the differences are few
She was quite innocent
But you are matured
Voluptuous and sensual
Onlookers allured
What is that hint
of desperation I see
It has not evaded or hidden
It is bothering me
I sense there is something
Lingering near your soul
That places you on the
Edge of losing control
Could it be life in general
Or a troubled past
Or a broken heart
That forever lasts
Whatever it may be
It is dampening your spirit
It's manipulating you
And keeping you near it
Your pulchritude so appealing
Inside and out
Should diminish any fears
Or hurt or doubt
Let go of the past
And walk toward the light
Your future continues
To be glaringly bright
Walk away from it's grasp
Just as you walked into this room
Elegant and poised
Whispering away any gloom

You unveiled an aura
When your essence escaped
When you walked in
In crimson light we were draped
Honored by your presence
Vying for your time
The introduction to you
The pleasure was all mine
I hope to see you
again very soon
As sure as the daybreak
And glow of the moon
If you are wondering how I could
describe you so intricately
The girl was you and the woman is me
Love Yourself

MY WHITE DRESS
In my white dress
Legs elongated and lean
Silver jewelry glistening
Crisp cool and clean
Strutting with my hand on hip
Like a runway walking beauty
Like beautiful is hastily slipping away
And to save it is my duty
Pristine elegant chignon
Hair slicked back and shining
Black as a star-filled night
Tasteful outside dining
Heads turn as I walk by
Male and female alike
It doesn't matter where I'm going
As long as I'm looking right

Then drop the hair and shake it
Doesn't matter if you bought it
They may have attended the luxurious hair class
But we're the ones who taught it
Go ahead and shake it, like a dancer performing on stage
Looking like a 20 year old beauty
At 44 years of age
Don't be afraid to show it ladies
My counterparts of 40 plus
Because we are the new 30
They ain't got nothin on us
Don't worry if the thighs are bigger
Or if the hips have spread s bit
The size 2 you see hanging on the rack
Ain't nobody wearing it
When your man holds you tight
He's happy his arms are full
That skinny is better and cuter
Is just a bunch of bull
Now I'm not knocking thin
It works for some, that's cool
But when you put on a few
He's looking don't be no fool
That you are no longer attractive
Don't buy it, you can get it for free
The media dishes it out everyday
Just grab the remote and turn on the tv
This is time honored beauty
What's known as the real thing
This body, this woman can carry life
A new person into the world bring
Birthed your children, nurtured you
Held you down when you were broke
Took up for you whenever

Someone negative about you spoke
Gave you love when she was tired
Because she knew you'd been working hard
Cooked your dinner washed the dishes
scrubbing and cleaning that left her scarred
All with love and devotion growing older
But all the work still waiting there
Still putting effort into looking pretty
Wanting you to know that she cares
So turn to her tell her she's beautiful
Both inside as well as out
That she's wanted desired and loved
Leave no inkling of a doubt
Let this woman of greater substance
know that she's still smoking hot
Appreciate all of her beauty
Because what you see is what you've got

SHADOWS

My compassion shadows me
Everywhere I go
Follows my forgiving heart
For everyone I know
It's invisible outline lumbers slowly
Searching for ways to care
Using caution as it approaches
In case someone fragile is there
Sometimes I wonder why my compassion
Is restless and cannot sleep
And then I realize it's because
There is so much pain I keep
Not for holding or dwelling in misery

But for remembrance of how it feels
To suffer heartache, tragedy, sickness
And unanswered mercy appeals
It knows so well the miracle of a child
And the anguish of losing one
The joys of finally living your dream
And holding a precious son
It knows of near death experiences
And almost leaving this world
Of living with tormented memories
Sanity tumbles unfurled
It knows the pleasure of being in love
Being hurt rejected and scorned
But also knows the euphoria of requite
Being treasured with lovers halo adorned
Of bedding in the arms of someone who loves you
For who you are and will come to be
Believes in you and your propensities
Letting you soar and your spirit fly free
But it also knows there are those that suffer
Are abused and mistreated beat down
Trapped behind doors that are closed to the world
Suffocating in despair they drown
Looking for a way to turn the wheel
Flow the tide in a different way
Hanging on to life and hope in their hearts
As they fight thru another day
My compassion will never allow me to forget
No matter how good things get for me
That for some only faith and belief is their savior
And for those thou mercy I plea
Pull together the fragments of their broken

hearts
Soothe their minds with peace and calm thought
Let them know that compassion shadows them
Fellow empathy that can not be bought
Love shadows the way to compassionate dreams
That become realities light
When others unselfishly shine in the dark
And attempt to change wrongs to right
Leading all souls to friendship and kisses
Of beauty loyalty and pride
Letting them see they have not been forgotten
And that you will never leave their side
Believe receive elevate and create
A path that leads the way
Filled with shadows of I love yous I miss yous
positive affirmations each day
Those of you with compassionate hearts
Teach your neighbor your friend your offspring
To love unceasingly be forgiving and trust
That good fruitage their actions will bring
How do you teach it? Just be it and then
Joy and delight will find it's way in
The ones that you touch will find the way
As your shadow appears at the dusk of day

TOMORROW ...

Is never promised we all know but it breathes the life of hope into our frail existence and carries the spirit when the body is weak. It holds the power of the sun destined to arise and shine the beacon of light through despair. It holds our desires and caresses the soul as it lays battered and bruised from life's journey. It opens eyes to the possibilities and closes them back when it's impossible, forwards the clock when life is unbearable and makes time stand still when the moment is immeasurable; gives true meaning to the smallest word and closes the door to a thoughtless act. It attracts dreams and empowers the mind, gives weight to a pounding heart's treasure and lightens it's burden when it's beat is distressed. It remembers the triumphs and melts away the disappointments ; let's bygones be bygones and makes way for new realities; Restores inner strength and rejuvenates determination, invents new love and adventure, rests weariness and moves closer to eternity.

It gives time it gives rest it gives power it gives wings it turns now into then and darkness into light sometimes makes wrongs...sometimes makes wrongs right. It blinds and believes and sometimes deceives. It calms it excites can soothe can ignite. It delivers and receives ; rejoices and even grieves. It loses and it wins finishes and begins. It emboldens and it wills, gives life and even kills; leaps heights unprecedented , plunges into depths never seen ; can decipher the most complex and explain what you mean. It can gently sway the breeze and ferociously stir the wind; shed light on the future, make peace with the end. It can cool with winter's chill and flame with boiling sun. It arrives just in time for many but never shows up for some....but the one thing it never does is.......fail to come

TODAY....

Has given me life and healing, hope for the future and rest from the past, love, friendship, disappointments and achievements, children to care for and a child of my own, my health good and bad; the opportunity to make amends and the wisdom and heart to deal with regrets, time to remember the past, to right fixable wrongs and apologize for those mistakes that I cannot change; Tears to weep for the losses and the joys, a heart filled with love and understanding for anyone who wants and needs it and even some that don't the will to move on and the desire to rekindle, the ability to reach my goals and the time to set more, the strength to never give up and the tenacity to say what I mean and do what I want; spiritual guidance to protect me from harm and allow me to have a relationship with my Creator, to worship and to be a good person and refine my heart. The tools to remember and reminisce, to hold things dear and close to my heart; to cry tears of pain and struggle with decision, to cultivate my talents and overcome my fears; being in love and loving deeply and sincerely, a constant struggle for faith, integrity and loyalty, a sinners constant plea, with flaws, blemishes, beauty and wrongs I'm grateful for being me; imagination and creativity daydreams and music, I can't forget music, I love it so much. It has gotten me through so many trials, triumphs, loves, heartaches, everything in my life....thank you for the gifts of love, creativity and music, they have almost made me complete. Today....... has given me so many things, almost everything...it just hasn't given me.....You

AWAKENED

Awaken my heart with trueness and love
Awaken my soul with the gift
Direct my footsteps to follow you
And my sunken countenance lift
I'm awakened in the morning
By the rising sun
And drifted to sleep by the moon
though never have I given thought to the air
I breathe or the sound when I hear a sweet tune
Awaken my desire to love unreservedly
Not holding back out of fear
No matter if someone returns it to me
The privilege of love I hold dear
For none of us deserve
The love we receive
It can not really be earned

There's no need to refrain from displaying it
Out of fear of being spurned
Open my eyes to see the beauty
Of every good thing around me
Allow me to know the real meaning of give
And the truthfulness that sets me free
Awaken my senses to feel the warmth
And to come in out of the cold
I want to appreciate my life
And live fully until I grow old
Thank you for all of your undeserved
kindness
Thank you for helping me believe
Thank you for everything that I have
And thank you for awakening me

OVERRATED
What is gained by moving on
Saving time? Becoming strong?
What does light mean to the dark?
Will it come back when there's no spark?
Why does rain equate gloomy and blue?
Doesn't it glisten when the light shines thru?
How does anger compare to pain?
Anger is fleeting the other remains
Leave your past behind they say
But isn't that what made you this way?
Should everything you did and everything
you knew
Be ignored the things that made this you?
Of course as you learn you grow and expand

But that's also what happens when food you demand
It's true we learn from our mistakes
But learning does not corrections make
To live in the past is to never grow
To remember your past is all you know
It's what you've been, where you are
What you've become and accomplished so far
It's remembering that helps you retain what you learned
To record your time and get paid what you earned
It's love lost that gives you the scars on your heart
Your battle wounds honor that you were a part
Of life in the past a mosaic of time
That passes us all by and stops on a dime
Only to tell you it's moving on
Will never come back to right any wrongs
What's done is done, What's been has been
Let tomorrow come, let come what may in
Renew who you are who you want to be
But don't lose you or try to become me
Take what you've learned and use it for good
To better your life and others you should
Look back sometimes and reminisce
But don't get stuck on what you missed
Embrace what you've had and fight for more
Never give up and swim for the shore
When you feel like your sinking and need a hand
Reach out for those in your past who stand
Forever by your side in thought or in deed

Will always be there when you're in need
New is good but old is not bad
When you forget where you come from
that's really sad
Dig deep to go further and stop and rest
On comfort from those that knew you best
When time is not honored and age not adored
Wisdom is lost and all that is stored
In time capsules buried in the sand
That will give no assistance if not in hand
Growing and learning should be appreciated
But forgetting your past is overrated

THE DISTANCE

So very far I have come
So very far I have to go
I'm weary and I'm tired
I'm ambitious and inspired
The road is long
Some things I've done wrong
Don't know where I belong
But I have to remain strong
So far to go
So far still
The things I won't do
The things I will
Will travel on this road until
I reach my destination
This is my revelation
That this human nation
And my emotional station
Requires translation
Of a variation

With trouble mine
Intervention divine
I will be fine
Thy heart refine
Travel this road
Continue with this load
Ambiguous frail, humble abode
Travel long
This endless song
Be with me
I need thee
Indefinitely
Cold and storm
Please keep me warm
Travel with me
I need thee
To cross a stream
Forging waters
Living a dream
Sons and daughters
Darkened cloud
Cry out loud
Rain falls
Nature calls
Ocean walls
Grow ever so high
Seeking the sky
Asking why
The journey is so long
Will I remain strong?
Have I done wrong?
Where do I belong?
The truth I seek
Restore the meek
Mountain peak
So far away

Endless day
From April 'til May
This prayer I say
Release my soul
To reach my goal
Troubled heart
A work of art
Intricate design
Trouble mine
Intervene divine
Make me fine
Thou heart you refine
Hot and rain
Help me refrain
From going insane
My faith remain
Give me shelter
Darkened night
Guiding light
To aid my sight
Struggle on
Pace your feet
Struggle on
Walk repeat
Marching fighter
Steps are quicker
Load is lighter
Thanksgiving from my soul
Love provider
Blessing me
Rebuild my heart
Help me make
A brand new start
Rest my soul
And continue on
Thru the night

Into the dawn
Make it there
I'm certain I will
My journey's map
My goal reveal
Darken the day
Lighten the night
Refuel my power
To fight the fight
Steps getting shorter
Steady pace
Refresh thyself
And run the race
This journey is so long
Please keep me strong
Don't want to do wrong
This is where I belong
I want to continue
With no resistance
Please give me the strength
To go the distance

I AM Pt. 3
I am not one
To trifle with
I'm not one to
Slap or hit
Tear me down
I'll walk away
Not even love
Can make
Me stay
I refuse to

Be mistreated
I refuse to cower
To fear your anger
To give you power
Over my soul
Over my mind
I am not
The weakened kind
I am confident
I am strong
My list of attributes
Is ten feet long
You can not break me
Don't even try
I'll pack my things
And tell you "bye"
Hold my hand
And walk with me
Encouragement, support
Is the key
Talk to me
Listen when I speak
Build me up
Make me feel complete
Be my other half
My strong broad arm
Kiss me with your compliments
Woo me with your charm
I'll do the same for you
I'll love you in return
But my love and trust
You'll have to earn
Then we can be part
Of something that lasts
Leave our troubled minds
In the past

Grow together
Become brand new
You respect me
And I'll respect you
I'll protect your heart
And you be my guard
Stand by each other
When times get hard
Fight off the monsters
Battle the beast
Be my hero
Make your wants the least
Put my needs first
Provide me with a home
That's loving and warm
A place of our own
That no one can take
Tear down or destroy
Filled with laughter
And sunshine and joy
Speak to me kindly
Consider my feelings
Show loving concern
In all of your dealings
Be honest and true
And honor my name
Give me your undivided attention
And I'll do the same
Surprise me with presents
Not big ones but small
The ones that show you thought it thru
And gave it your all
Always console me
When I am sad
Tell me I'm the best thing
You ever had

Make me the reason
You go to work each day
The reason you come home
The reason you stay
Carry my burdens
Don't be the load
Be willing to say "I'm sorry"
When apologies are owed
Let me be myself
I'll nurture your talents
Support your desires
Give our life balance
Express yourself
Don't hold it in side
Let m be the one
In which you confide
Tell me your secrets
Good ones and bad
Share the thing that make you happy
The ones that make you sad
Take me out to dinner
Say "you don't have to cook"
Sit close to me on the couch
While I'm reading a book
Whisper in my ear
Kiss me on the cheek
Stare into my eyes
When they're no words to speak
Hold my hand
When I'm nervous and scared
When I'm tired and weary
When it seems no one else cared
Give me the reassurance
That you'll always be around
That you can break my fall
Without making a sound

That you will have my back
No matter what takes place
When I'm feeling empty
Fill up the space
These are the things that I require
Request, ask for, pray and desire
I'm a reasonable woman
I am reliable and smart
I resolve with my mind
And give with my heart
I am mature, patient,
Pleasant and fun
But if you're looking for a doormat
I am not the one

CAROLINA GIRL

So much to do, so little time
Ready to expand, ready to rhyme
Running for the border, heading to the Tre'
Where she grew up running everyday
Water in the creek, dirt on the field
All the possibilities ready to reap the yield
Always moving forward but not afraid to look back
Hear the train whistle, I'm only minutes from the track
Plane engines roaring, horses trotting by
Urban meets country and December meets July
All over town the air is speaking fast
Filled with friends and laughter, wish it all would last
Football games, baseball, basketball cheers
Carry hopes and dreams that will last

throughout the years
Hiding from reality, hoping for a dream
Things will get better no matter how bad it may seem
Struggling for good grades, fighting for a spot
Dressing to impress , looking smoking hot
Designer jeans and labels, cruising around in the car
Giggling with best friends, madly in love with the football star
Kisses in the stairwell, precious hugs goodbye
Sneaking into class late, teacher asking why
Ready for the world but afraid of what will come
Success there for many and stardom for some
Teaching family values, passing down tradition
Living life that's golden and everybody missing
Blowing kisses in the air as changing times bring pain and glory
One of many lights in the southern living story
Colorful tulips bloom, springtime gone too soon
Blossoming dogwood trees can bring you to your knees
Luscious beautiful green , the best you've ever seen
But ain't nothing in the world like a Carolina Girl

SOLACE

Comfort in sorrow, misfortune, or trouble;
alleviation of distress or discomfort.
Who will comfort me?
Is it thee, do you hear my plea?
I'm in trouble, in need of solace, a place to
hide, a place to confide
& I have not found it. You are too busy &
blind to my need,
the anger in my heart my prayers impede.
I know he hears but these are my fears,
that when I am so wrong, he will no longer
listen. See if you listen hold my hand you
can make me understand that all is forgiven
all is right, all you can do is survive the
night.
Honor my value & make me believe that
everything will be okay, I will live to see
another day.
something that gives comfort, consolation,
or relief. Who is this Consolation thief?
Console, control are one in the same,
inconsolable, uncontrollable is my name.
Forgive the former, thine heart is filled with
the blood of torture & innocence killed
slaughtered on the ground washed with time,
solace will ever never be mine
to comfort, console, or cheer (a person,
oneself, the heart, this is the way my healing
will start,
find my happiness my humor & lighthearted
sails, that drift on the ocean & evil expels,
I am a child of yesterday, I was not meant to
be this way.

Pride & determination are my brothers
forgiveness & acceptance my nurturing mothers
& they taught me to beg for what I deserve
humble thyself to the God I serve,
on these damaged knees I kneel and pray...help me know just what to say , hold my hand in my solitude, help me find my pulchritude
aged as it may be care not I as long as it emanates from inside
to alleviate or relieve sorrow, distress, someone help me out of this mess
I don't know who I am anymore, I hope when I begin to recognize myself,
She is someone that I like, no someone that I love, someone that I want to love
Speak the words that haunt us afraid to see what is deep inside of me
Trouble heart speak the truth, it is your only solace

FOR THOSE THAT WANT TO FIND THEMSELVES BUT DON'T KNOW WHERE TO LOOK
Become a novel an autobiography, a virtual open book
Use the stars as a guide, north west, south or east
Make your fears, your apprehensions, your doubts the very least
Don't runaway, don't run away, stand and feel the rage

Let go of inhibitions, release courage from it's cage
Inside your dreams, outside your feelings open and exposed
Walk toward the future, embrace the present, the doors to the past are closed

SUPERFICIAL

If you only look at the surface you will never know the whole story
You are unable to see inside thru the triumphs thru the failures and the glory
She's gorgeous yet she's angry she' has hatred in her heart
Gold digging and murderous being, will tear your life apart
He's aged but he' is humble, his honor earned and decreed
But all you can see is dollar signs and wealthy thru your greed
She is voluptuous and curvy, ample full and spread
Beautiful mind and integrity charmed and gracious born and bred
But all you see is heavy, not a show piece for all to see
Afraid to knock down the barriers and cross the shallow sea
Her hair is short and brittle not long and soft and flowing
Because she's fought thru chemotherapy is the truth that you're not knowing
Her fortitude is strong, stable as a brick wall
For all that she has been thru, nothing has

made her fall
Knocked around and beaten by trouble tragedy and strife
All you see is weak and weary but she would make the perfect wife
He is short and basic, no flash no rich lifestyle
But all you really want to do is trick him and beguile
But he would love you forever, by your side support & adore
But you can't see past his height you think that you want so much more
She wants to be your friend, stand by you and you comfort bring
You look at outside appearances and feel she doesn't need a thing
But if you listen to her heart speak you will know she needs your shoulder
On the verge of committing suicide no desire to grow any older
He's reaching out his hand to you, looking for it so he can hold
Get comfort from your warmth but the coldness leaves stories untold
On the surface you don't see someone sick and weakening from disease
Bloated by medicine and procedures holding on because of weakened knees
Look into people's eyes, listen to the sound of a voice
Sincerely take a moment to make a wiser choice
Really who isn't someone that deserves the time it takes
To see past the facade and layers that

struggle and hard life makes
Care enough to consider the feelings other
than your own
You will never know when you need it when
you're feeling all alone
Experience isn't the only teacher time and
love teach us as well
What's inside of someone's mind and heart
you can't really tell
Unless you use precious minutes to affect a
more precious friend
You can heal a broken heart, help an open
wound to mend
Don't be afraid to believe, in this world that
is vicious and mean
Because the very thing you will miss is the
goodness that goes unseen

WHO YOU ARE

You are who you think you are
You are everything and more
It is not imagination
Or visions of grandeur
You have the propensity
To be the favored one
Unique and mysterious
Your journey has just begun
You are what you feel
Be it positive or not
Remember to always believe in your self
For you are all you've got
You are the way you show yourself
What you see is what you get

Show the world you are here to shine
and that you ain't seen nothing yet
What you are not is what others assume
That is their perception of you
You don't have to accept that label
Or engage what they want you to do
Only you really know your capabilities
Only you know how you truly feel
Follow your dreams, remain true to yourself
When you are ready to show and reveal
Then Give 'em what you got
Grab on & hold on tight
Whatever gets in your way
Be prepared to scratch and fight
Dream big or not at all
Make it worth the wait
Be prepared to knock down walls
Keep all of your priorities straight
If anyone speaks negatively to you
Don't allow it to be discouraging
There are those that have no ambition
So your goals they like disparaging
Most importantly, live a meaningful life
Follow your dreams with no regret
Leave an indelible print
That the world will never forget

SUPERFICIAL Pt.2
Superficial and shallow is obtuse
It is not desirable or honorable
Dig deeper, climb steeper
Search for what is fulfilling, not full
Full of empty and nothing
Don't you want something
That is cherished priceless and real

Don't hide behind bravado
Expose how you truly feel
You can only wade in shallow waters
Sparse and incapable of immersion
Look past the facade of a person's outer shell
Hold out for the authentic version
Swim deep in the ocean of abandon
Baptize your fears in the sea of openness
Free yourself of stereotypes and patent labels
It is the only way to find true happiness
Dig deep until you find the bottom of a soul
Find the treasure and the wealth of pleasurable being
Earn the trust of one you love and build their faith in who you are and they will slowly show you things that you're not seeing
Beauty is what you behold though not only with your eyes, but with your heart and your mind and your soul
Look within, show inside, your true self do not hide
Be yourself and do not play a role
It is inevitable that what you will get in return is emptiness
Incapable of soaring, unable to sail
A relationship based on nothing will be nothing, will do nothing, will surely fail
Superficial is not super; it is deflated, emaciated, unrelated, demonstrated desolation, a useless creation of a shallow being, that wants to be whole but doesn't know how, so always taking a bow; puts on a show day after day with curtain calls and encores, leaving the stage with a smile but

behind closed doors, it weeps

POETRY IN MOTION

She moves mountains like the average man moves coals
She pushes boulders out of the way of her goals
She is poetry in motion when she walks
And everybody listens when she talks
She is love and the epitome of style and grace
Joy and contentment emanate beams from her face
She is desired but will never settle for less
With her knowledge and intelligence she can bless
She can comfort, she can soothe, she gives hope
She has a wide and expansive outlook scope
With positivity her enlightenment is her gift
When you hear her your countenance will lift
Because her sweet and melodic rhythmical voice
Makes the flowers bloom and tree branches rejoice
She is emotional and caring thru her strength
She carries burdens and hardships of any length
She can laugh, she can scream, she can cry
She is her, she is we, she's you and I
Don't betray her, don't neglect or disrespect
Her kind heart and her feelings you should protect

She's forgiving, she has patience, she is free
She's a woman who is you, who is me
Her life is poetry in motion, it's her story
Watch for her as she arrives in her glory

THE ANSWER

If love is the answer, what is the question
Is it truly the way or just a suggestion
If truth is light, what is the dark
If lies breed distrust, does honesty spark
If hate is a disease, what is the cure
Will it end our existence, and destroy what is pure
The ponder is always which is good which is bad
What is wrong what is right, what is happy or sad
My heart tells me one thing, my mind says another
Do I listen to one and ignore the other
If my eyes are the windows to the essence of me
Are my ears the pathway, will they help me to see
When I listen to the voice of the one I believe
Do they embrace falsehood, is it me they deceive?
If the ground that I walk on is solid and strong
Forgiveness corrects me when I'm involved in wrong
Determination guides my steps when I am weak
and paints a picture of my words when I'm

unable to speak
When my tears are falling, do they drown the pain
Does the laughter of joy keep me from going insane
If contentment is the door, is patience the key
When I'm lonely and broken is it hopeless for me
If chastity is my virtue, is desire a snare
When someone really loves you, is your protection the care
If tomorrow is not promised, is yesterday a lie
When someone leaves you, is it really goodbye
Or will you always be linked to the chain of their jail
Behind bars in their prison and doomed for a fail
The love in my heart is an anchor to my dreams
The nemesis of my serenity as strange as it seems
Love is the answer but the question is who
Because unfortunately I'm hopelessly in love with you

THOUGHTS ON AN UNBRIDLED TONGUE
It is not always what you say sometimes it is what you do
That defines the real person that lives inside

of you
It may not be what you do but what you say
That makes a person feel a certain way
We learned that sticks & stones can break our bones
But names will never hurt us
But telling that to a child that's called a derogatory name
May be considered cold & callous
Or a woman that's called outside of her name
Would agree that it is degrading
To say something vile just because you're upset
Proves that the milk of human kindness is fading
To speak or act in a manner that is hurtful
Is undignified, disenchanting & of no benefit
Just because you have the right to say something
Does not make it proper, ethical or appropriate
Disrespect that is rampant & anger uncontrolled
Is uncivilized and a disservice to our youth
Be the type of person that you want them to be
Be kind, be considerate, speak the truth
Don't hide behind your rights & your views
Don't berate just because you do not agree
Be mindful of who you speak to with a vicious tongue
And be careful how you talk to me
You see I love hard & strong & I feel with my heart

I forgive & I have compassion for everyone
But if I'm not treated with dignity, respect or honor
I will walk away after all is said & done
Just remember that we all belong in this space
& we must share it whether we delight or contrast
Think before you act, keep some thoughts to yourself
Leave the trifle & foolish in the past
Don't post mean pictures, you know it's wrong
You shouldn't have to be told
But I will because it needs to be said
Stop acting like you're two years old!
Remember what mama told you about what you say
If it's not nice say nothing at all
Revere each law abider as you stand side by side
Not forgetting that pride layeth before a fall

QUEEN
I walk with the sun, I run with the moon, I sit with the stars in the sky
I fall with the rain, a breeze in the wind ; a castle of poetry have I
My confidence reigns, my courage directs, My peace fills my kingdom with joy
I'm one with the sea and basking on the shore of a nation
A child of love and of passion's creation

I rule with a scepter of iron and gold
My heart is my atlas and guide
I leap with the leopards and cry with doves
In the mountains of contentment I reside
My dreams are my subjects, my aspirations my court
My ladies in waiting are my means of support
My king is my serenity, my Lord of Divinity
Is my lawgiver, my honored, my protection
There is no fear of want, no longing or need
My praises are my displays of affection
My reed of respect is wielded with compassion
My crown is my beauty and my glory
My robe royal crimson, trimmed in fine gold
Are my words, as I tell my story
I'm humbled by life by love and desire
By heights that I never will reach
My vow is to give and take nothing in return
To empower, inspire and teach
No bow or a curtsy, no kneeling or pose
Is expected or demanded from me
Distinguished and regal, yet a servant of my brethren
Is who I will always be

THE TOP
I'm on top of a mountain standing tall and strong
The stirring whirling winds are singing their

happy song

Bright clear and shining after the raging storm
Will strongly stand my ground when the clouds begin to form
Look at the sky and declare I'm free
No more rain dampening me
My voice reverberates as I cry out loud
My head lifted up stature tall and proud
The beaming of my face the tears in my eyes
Reflect the appreciation for the lows and the highs
I've been at the bottom but refused to stay there
My heart broken and shattered my soul unaware
That beyond the horizon a mountain stood
To climb from the depths to reach the good
The strength to enable a lengthy climb
Struggle that seemed like unending time
To never give up to extinguish the doubt
To protect the mind and peace be without
Holding on to faith and hope hat has dwindled
When your loving existence has yet to be kindled
The will to hang on I endured the pain
From hate and bitterness I chose to refrain
Engaged in the climb slowly reaching the peak
My breathing labored I'm unable to speak
The wind often helping me sometimes pushing me off track
Held on for dear life I refused to look back
I kept my grip tight hands burning and bleeding

Still focused on the top and the One that was leading
The air became thinner the sun became warm
Getting closer to the top watching radiant clouds form
The moment of truth so frail and afraid
Let not this climb be in vain I prayed
My heart fluttering my strength renewed
I peered over the top and gratefully viewed
The beauty before me the tears would not stop
I had finally reached The Top

I'VE LEARNED.....
That when your heart is filled with love
There is no room for hate
When you desire love in return
Sometimes you have to wait
When love is overwhelming
It fills your cup
It fuels you to move forward
And never give up
It forgives all debts
And ends all doubt
Slowly but surely
It works things out
You may not understand
Where it's going
But at the end you realize
You were better off not knowing
Because where you've been
Is what teaches you how

To deal with the future
And to get thru the now

STACY

Always been there for me
She is unmistakably
The best friend anyone could be
Words cannot express
What she means
We've been best friends
Since we were teens
Ways to describe her;
Loyal loving kind and sweet
Like Berries on the vine
Let me take this time to tell you
About this friend of mine
encouraging inspiring positive spirit
Timeless ageless beauty
To stand by me
And have my back
She feels it is her duty
Never mean to me
Understands me
Always on my side
When I'm feeling vulnerable
She's my place to hide
She's my strength when I am weak
Talks for me when I can't speak
My eyes for me when I can't see
Ears for me when I don't hear
Whenever I need her the most
She will automatically appear
She hears my voice when there's no sound
My releaser when I need to be free

It doesn't matter what it is
She's whatever I need her to be
She's my match when I need to light a fire
My water when I need to put one out
Even when I can't express myself
She knows what I'm talking about
Like the time I thought I was losing my mind
She came and sat with me
Looked into my eyes and said
"This is how it needs to be,
Hold your head up high my friend
Don't ever look down again
Things are gonna work out for you
Just trust in our God's plan"
She didn't even know that I needed her
But as usual she appeared
Held my hand and let me know
There was nothing to be feared
There has never been a time in life
That I couldn't depend on her love
It's like she was made to be my friend
A gift from God above
She's my sun when I need the light
When I'm weak she is my power
She's a garden grown in springtime
A beautiful blossoming flower
She's helped me become who I need to be
But loved me not requiring a change
Not matter what age or time in my life
Even if I'm acting strange
Never held anything against me
Simply loves me for who I am
Never forgot important days
Goes to bat when I'm in a jam
She pinch hits when I'm not able to swing

Stands in when I can't play the part
Holds my hand when I'm scared and afraid
When I'm hurt she protects my heart
"And what do I do for her?" you might ask
Well I can say to that
For everything she's does for me
I've matched it tit for tat
It's not that friends should keep a score
Or return a deed for a deed
It's just that I will always be there
Whenever she's in need
She always known I would be there
Like when we were in high school
Always riding shotgun
Thinking we were cool
Growing up together
Disappointments and success
Trying to stay out of trouble
In the middle of a mess
Blocking blows thrown at us
Never giving up the fight
Grateful for all we receive
And praying every night
Thanking God for each other
Praying for the one that's under a test
One can always help the other
Because we know each other best
Love romance and heartbreaks
Marriage and giving birth
Raising our children and hoping
A better future for this earth
We haven't always been together
Divided by borders and time
But there's always a reflective mirror
Like a friendship shadow mime
I'm the carrier of her crown, the Queen

Her throne because she's royalty
She will always have my undying love
And my heartfelt loyalty
I feel I've been blessed with this gift
And I treasure her like she is gold
Diamonds rubies and precious gems
Best friends 'til we're 100 years old
And before I take my last dying breath
I will turn to see her face
I already know she'll be there
In her usual time honored place
She will be there by my side
As she's forever and always been
And I will turn and say to her
"My life long sweet dear friend,
I love you; You have been to me
What no one else could achieve
Always holding on for me
Even when I didn't believe;
I've always tried to be
The friend that you deserve
That's why in this last act of love
I'm ready here to serve
As your replacement on this deathbed
With everlasting time in view
I'm putting myself here in your place
I would give my life for you

THE SULLEN PLIGHT OF THE UNBELIEVERS
Wild-eyed and dangerous, fortitude not kept, struggling onward, unbelievable passion,

raging bull caged and waiting to destroy
Dead inside, feeling nothing, lonesome love,
compassion abducted
Rush of warmth, plunged in a valley of
ravenous wolves and amorous clover,
painted green with red stained sorrow,
slumped in defeat, surrendered posture, light
thy countenance with a drop of sun,
graciously clutched extremities, tangled and
intertwined, wanting for nothing, needing
everything, invisible to the world yet seen
by all, pride is before a fall, pride layeth
before a fall. Wanting to believe, nothing to
hold on to, downward spiral, grasping at the
air, weightless, mindless, faulted being,
reach for me, believe. Transparent existence,
shredded hope, pointed weapon, angled
scope, rising slowly, weakened knees, pull
me up, help me please. Lengthened night
when will daylight come, why does it shine
for only some, ransomed hope belie my
happiness, indigent, broken unable to pay,
wealthy counterparts giveth coins thy beg,
reimburse my captors, thou mercy I pray.
Fail me not dearest, honored loved one, heal
thy affection with a kiss of amber, water thy
emptiness with bastioned deluge, In dancer's
pose my body camber. Rise to feel the
nested hold, making me lovable, courageous
and bold, sheddeth light on darkness and
dreams turned to nightmares in impish
gleams, hold me steady, balanced and still,
able to emanate tenderheartedness at will.
Happiness fill the damaged heart,
effervescent colloquy impart. Rigorous
restoring of failing fettle, trembling fear and

uneasiness settle. Coy existence void of pleasure and delight, sorrowful duration of this malevolent plight. Banished from softness, cavernous soul, abrasive exterior black like coal. Feelers numbed with time and age, sprinkled with disdain and vicious rage. Pilfered life irretrievably swept into steel laden vaults where aspiration is kept. Melodies written by bewildered composers, performed by untalented euphonic opposed. Dig us out from these desolate graves, deep in brumal, aphotic caves. Out of the earth in bedraggled trough to places plush, comfortable and soft. Show us agreeable favored
expression, and the value of open, honest confession. Righteous resolve to assist the deprived from those that have prospered, held on and survived. Reach out for those that are broken in spirit, the cries of the lowly determinedly hear it. Randomly giving overachievers, gifted harmonious humane receivers, faithful chosen ones favored and hired, wholesome, valued, altruistic inspired. I beg of help and sadness relievers for the sullen plight of the unbelievers.

THE LOVELY ONES
Randomly seeking, finding intention
Clandestine pursuit too secret to mention
Beautiful skin and glistening eyes
Browned by the sun , washed with tears

Curvaceous shell, flirtatious nature
Your secrets tell of the mysterious club
That struts around with countenance high
Heads turn as they walk by, but what's inside
The lovely shell, enlighten us your secrets tell
What is this way you walk around carried
By lovely limbs, what is behind those eyes
Under that flowing dark hair and perfectly
Bronzed skin? Oh lovely ones please let us in
Verify the lovely feelings of popularity and
Social clarity, rounded hips and full plump lips
Holding on to lovely arms delicately placing
Each dainty step, legs extend like graceful clks
Neck elongated, back smooth and sleek
What is this existence of which you speak?
What is the origin of the natural glow and
omnipresent elegance, swaddled in such prettiness?
Is there honor or only golden hues
Happy beginnings with unpleasant endings
Where are you going? Where will you be?
I need you to stand there and look pretty for me

THE STOLEN HEART
My heart was stolen long ago
Pilfered right in front of my face
I can describe the person who stole it

And give the exact time and place
All I could do was stand there
And watch them run away
And hope they would return it to me
But they haven't until this day
And I didn't report it stolen
For it was like I was an accomplice
Complicit willing and enabling
Somehow involved in this
The perpetrator soon returned
To the scene of the crime to take
Whatever remained of my dignity
And further a fool of me make
How could my heart betray me
Going willingly not putting up a fight
Being lulled into a sense of security
And dragged off into the night
At first I cried at the loss
and vowed to get my heart back
But whenever I would get close
The courage I would lack
So I decided to steal one myself
From the one that had stolen from me
Determined that thief would surely feel
How living without one would be
I succeeded but it wasn't worth the hurt
That was caused by the lack of a beat
Without my own heart to receive it
All I could feel was defeat
There they were holding my heart
And there I was holding one too
Both of us standing there useless
And not knowing what to do
Both refusing to give back
What we knew belonged to the other
Holding on as if for dear life

So afraid it would be snatched by another
Not wanting to let go and give in
Our lives destined for severe heartache
Discovering how painful it is
When you don't give and only take
Stubbornly we never exchanged
Or gave back what belonged rightfully
To the other so that it could be used
To love someone else faithfully
A life sentence of confusion and pain
Why couldn't we just compromise
The desperate love we once had
Has caused us to start to despise
One another and all that we hold close
Because we stole and had no regret
Our punishment is remembering the love
Never being able to forget
To fall in love don't steal someone's heart
Let them keep theirs and you keep yours
And when they leave, let them go
And lock all your windows and doors

SUITCASE

On my way to life, a trip that's long overdue
Packed my bags and leaving, I'm coming home to you
All I have left in my suitcase, is everything that I own
My load is light, I'm on my way, I'm traveling alone
The past mistakes behind me, the present is where I dwell
I know not what the future holds, only time will tell
The journey may be long, labored, slow but

sure
There is nothing I will come up against that I cannot endure
I have lived thru many heartaches, I have suffered and I have lost
I have paid the price for existing no matter how great the cost
The dues are paid, I am elevating to new heights that I have earned
I take with me the hope of new and all that I have learned
The storms have left me homeless, killed my loved ones and some friends
The pain, I carry it with me, for that part never ends
But after time and trials, triumph and defeat
I have chosen to learn the lesson of things I won't repeat
My body has been broken, it has been battered, scarred & its worn
But I believe I have a purpose, the reason I was born
I have loved and lost and plummeted into depths of sadness and gloom
But I have also loved and won, been swept with passion's broom
I have bad memories that live in my being, they sometimes torture my fragile mind
But I have good ones that take over and force them to move behind
"Let her live", they command as they choke them until they are out of air
"Leave her be, the torment is over; we will make her unaware
That in the shackles of her mind, sits misery held in jail

Bound and gagged forever, sentenced to
weep and wail
She will weep for the things she lost, wail
for the people that have deceased
But she will suffer no more for aged
tragedy, the former has been released"
I have grown to knowledge, have risen to
wisdom and to elevation of thought
As I am finding my way home, no foolish
dealings will be brought
I bring me and what I had left, when the dust
settled and I looked around
When life's tragedies were over, not all that
was lost was found
So I packed it in my bag, what was left and
what would fit
All things unneeded and trifle I refused to
carry it
I am almost there, I am coming, I am
coming home to love you
Take care and lavishly bathe in compassion
is what I am prepared to do
I will give you all that you need, it is your
time to be happy and free
I am ready to greet you and embrace , I am
ready to meet the new me

MY MOTHER'S EARRINGS

My mother's earrings
Dangling and glistening
Her pretty face in the light
Her quiet power lingers in her voice
A little girl enamored by her pretty dress
Enthralled with her intelligence

And ability to make me smile
Always able to make everything alright
Expelling fears in the night with a kiss
Three times she pecks my cheek
And I drift into dreaming
In the morning awakened by her laughter
And the smell of her cooking
Getting ready for school, gathering my books
She tells me goodbye and to be good
My packed lunch prepared by her loving hands
Reminds me of her and our unconditional love
She takes me to worship, she teaches me to pray,
Something that will stay with me forever
Listening patiently, encouraging always believing that things can be better
Enduring, long-suffering uplifting, honest and straightforward
Sharing her beauty, withholding nothing gave me what I'm working with
Taught me to work it out, taught me to walk away and do it for myself
Be pretty inside and out, reflect on what you learned , act like you had a mother that taught you how to act, call me when you need me I'll always be there, letting go of her apron strings I'm empowered to be beautiful, benevolent and bold
As I watch her earrings sparkle and I'm reminded that she
Taught me how to love

DEVOTION

Tattoo my name across your heart
And I'll put yours on mine
I'll make my hand fit into yours
And we will be just fine
I'll write your name across the sky
Put the stars on as a seal
Tell the sun to shine on you
So the love I have you feel
Tell the moon to light my path
So I can see the way
To get to you and feel your arms
Around me everyday
Tell the clouds to hold back the rain
And wait to fall at night
So we can hear the raindrops
And know everything's alright
Let the snow fall down on us
Surround us with it's chill
Let the oceans surround us
And with our teardrops fill
As we weep with joy they'll never run dry
For the rivers will carry us thru
To ponds of love and lakes of passion
Named after me and you
Write your promise on the back of my neck
And seal it with a kiss
I'll carry your burdens on my back
And I will promise you this
I'll always be there for you
You have a seal stamped on my heart
We'll be together thru the end
Not even death could tear us apart
Light the sky to tell the world
The fulfillment of you and I
And I will set this world on fire

If you ever say goodbye
Tell the mountains to rise for us
The hills to show their glory
For us and for our unending devotion
Our beautiful love story

LETTER TO MY FRIEND

Dear Friend, how are you feeling?
Are your feelings good like mine?
I hope this letter finds you happy
And everything in your life is in line
I haven't seen you in so long
I have missed you so, you have been crossing my mind
Your love and friendship I cherish,
You have always been so kind
Yesterday as I wrote this
I thought of the first time we met
Laughing and getting along
From the start our bond was set
You were honorable, trustworthy and loyal
Never turning your back on me
You were the one that I could turn to
For whatever the need may be
We have had a long distance friendship
We do not always keep in touch
But if needed we both would be there
We love each other very much

A letter of appreciation
Is what this is meant to be
I do not want more time to go by
Without you hearing from me
Life is short and precious
The time goes by very fast
Before you know, the days have gone by
And many years have passed
There is nothing that I want from you
Only for our friendship to stay alive
To last until there is no more time
To grow stronger, mature & thrive
If there is anything that you need from me
Please don't hesitate to ask
If I am capable, it is done
No matter what the task
Please know that I have missed you
And that you have a place in my heart
Forever indelibly etched
Like precious valuable art
Forgive me if I have not been there
If you needed a shoulder for tears
I promise it was not my intention
My dear friend of so many years
For all you had to do was call
I would have hurried to your side
I would have climbed the highest mountain
And faced the strongest tide
Many things have happened to me
There has been good and some have been bad
I am sure it is the same for you
Joyous times and unpleasant you've had
While of one thing I am quite sure
We both still exist on this earth
Still living this life we have been given

Receiving blessings beginning with birth
Aged and matured we may be
For that I am filled with grace
For the alternative would mean we were lost
Unable to reunite and embrace
Just remember to call my name
Should you need me or just want me here
I will always come when you call
If you reach out then I will appear
So long treasured friend, sincerely
I send this with love and with care
Receive this with the hugs I am enclosing
as if I was standing right there

TROUBLED HEART

Trouble heart, oh problem child
Make me humble meek and mild
Amber light, crimson glow
Tell me what I need to know
No insane nor enraged beast
Can devour a blessed feast
Mine it is, no one can take
A mockery of my sorrow make
Beat as drums, as tambourine rattle
Cause me anguish and make me addle
Pulchritude as vision seen
Reveals to me of what it means
Captured by this trouble mine
Self withhold and thus define
My lofty place thus abdicated
The wisdom of pain my loss created
Weathered terror, diminished pride
Now venomous words and hatred reside
Dwell in crevices, dark and cold
Yellowed, dingy, dirty and old

Uneducated thoughtless mind
Luring, seducing to be it's kind
"Follow me", it whispers, "come along
Join the forces of indecent and wrong"
I will not go, I'll follow the light
The army of truth and everything right
Silence heart, stifle reproach
Do not into my good nature encroach
Concentrate on healing and being good
Behave the way you know you should
Stay out of trouble, from behind the bars
Leaving gaping wounds and scars
Trial by jury, convicted to prison
Up from the ashes your torment has risen
Banish the rage, run away from revenge
Nurse the burns from fiery singe
Wait for love oh trouble one
Wait for morning dew and sun
Passed down for centuries thru generations
Damaging bonds and dividing nations
Family inheritance plundered and wasted
Once the bitterness of love is tasted
Disloyal friend your opposite faces
Double-crossing and backwards laces
Tie up my hands and bind my extremes
No matter how melodious it seems
It's song is toneless and sings off key
Troubling, torturing and deafening me

AMBER
Golden hues move in circles
Mesmerize and quiet the soul

Dripping softly yellow raindrops
Drizzle into a bottomless hole
Radiant sparkle, diamonds shine
Glistening twinkles blind the eyes
And warm the hands with fingertip touches
Hold me tightly, hold me tightly
Courageous shield made of stone
Preserving life from grievous design
Distinguishable only by mellow color
What is yours and what is mine
Heating embers growing faint
Shallow existence fading away
I beg to see you once again
Quiet my mind, quiet my mind
Lowly, lowly deepest care
Trailed me here and dropped flower petals
So I can find my way back home
Thru copper fields and trees with metals
Echo, echo hear the voice
In the wind softly blowing
Filling the air with buttercup scent
Rocking me to sleep, drowsy willow
Hold me close, hold me close
Near me, far way, far away nearness
Trickle teardrops, flow your way
Slow my breathing into deep
unconsciousness
Thru the night into the day
Crackle wood chips flamed in passion
Clash with the stars, direct your orchestra
Crescendo into suspenseful moment
My sweet amber, my sweet amber
I love you though I shall not speak
The faint of heart can only survive
Empty existence, craved indifference
Daring me to stay alive

Tribal colors royal reds
Crimson purple Lavender green
Thru the fog and endless clouds
Before the naked eye unseen
Transparent waves
Dampen crystal sands
Breathing new life
Into idle hands
Restoring color
To empty hues
Yellow autumn
Winter blues
Amber's light in the distance
Clay horizon
Sparkle rain
Diamond stars surround pearly moon
Echoes in the wind remain
Rocks me gently to rest and dream
Quietly trickle the flowing stream
Oh sweet amber hold me tightly
Quiet my mind, quiet my mind

EVILITY
No longer lurking , bold and brazen fool
Animalistic movements monstrous capabilities
Why don't you use your power for good?
Or at least assault one another
Where does the evil in you come from
Is it because you had no mother?
Yes you have a mother a father a daughter a son
Your family is the demonic and your proud

to be as one
You're heartless mindless and vicious
Just like your father the lie
And just like your ancestral counterparts
you will surely die
You hurt and kill and torture
Bully like the Nephelim of old
Your father tells you to torment
And you do what you are told
You think you have the mastery
But you have no authority
Just as your cowardly exit
During the flood you chose to flee
You couldn't go back to heaven
God wouldn't allow you there
You had proven your disloyalty
And complicit choice not to care
You followed someone that was rebellious
You chose to betray the Most High
There is no lower position
Even though you can ascend to the sky
But you can go no further
Than the naked eye can see
You're trapped in your own prison
You reside in evility
Those that are careless let you use them
Imperfection isn't enough
It's added to hardheartedness
And creates a ruthless cuff
Such trouble in the world
Such cruelty randomly dealt
Makes a humble loving heart
Suffer the pain that's felt
You don't deserve attention
This prose is not for you
It's a warning to the unguarded

A lesson in what to do
Guard your heart from badness
Hate it loath it's existence
Treat it like the pariah it is
Fight it's pull with all resistance
It's sneaky and cunning and sly
Will try to trick your mind
Make you think that it's acceptable
And leave the good behind
Don't be afraid of it's dark power
Because it is nowhere near a match
For your loving heavenly Father
To his arm yourself attach
Just like you would as a child
When you were scared and and comfort needed
He will take hold of you if his words are faithfully heeded
He'll envelop you with love, protection and the peace
That excels all thought and deed a haven for release
This outcast disposed community
Of everything that's vile
Disgusting filthy and poisonous
And determined to beguile
The havoc it wreaks is hurtful
But can be reversed in completion
Our Father has the power and
The willingness to give repletion
Of everything that's wholesome, lovable, chaste and true
The downtrodden he will uplift broken hearts he will renew
You can touch the warmth of the sun and drink the coolness of rain

Damages will be repaired interiors freed of pain
Guided by the twinkle of stars and the glowing light of the moon
The Creator of them all will save us and will relieve us very soon
Protect your heart with the shield of faith and your mind with the helmet of salvation
Equipped with the sword of the spirit and righteous indignation
Nourished by spiritual feedings sustained by honorable staff
Sifting thru the weeds and blowing away the chaff
Your countenance lit with hope and strengthened to walk without fear
Hold your heads erect for our deliverance is near

JUDGING AT THE WHEAT FIELD
Standing on the golden plain
Orange in the horizon
Wonder on my imagination
Simplistic form at rest
The will I release to the wind
That fondles my fragile hairs
Numbered are the days of grain
The harvest near at hand
Where will I be tomorrow
When winter turns the corner
Rushing to beat the aphid
Begging a settle of calm?
The chaff dances in the air
Orchestra bales and cowbell quartets
Filtering strawberry symphonies

Daisies kneel in prayer
Giving thanks for a cleansing shower
Chimes are in the distance
Hammer heads drown pleasantries
Glory days are ending
There exist no more of these
What did I do and why?
Was it a necessary evil?
Or it could have been a good one
A replenishment of the soul
This good deed has to be punished
None ever escapes the wrath
Let it be swift and merciful touch
Withstand and release last breath
Surrender with infinite counting
Rainbow will follow a storm
Wrap yourself in it's colors
What is the color of light?
Golden green transparent?
As the moisture rises to praise
Then retreats to it's earthly abode
Never to occur again
Agony is not sweet or soft
Rain wash away my sins
Making me glow with purity
As The dawn of a new day begins

EULOGY
I'm so sorry that you're gone
I will miss you so very much
Your deep searching dark brown eyes

Your precious loving touch
I'll miss your soothing voice
Your proclamations of love
That the you I knew before is gone
I'm painfully aware of
The stages of grief are troubling
They have no mercy on the mournful
They go from depressed and denial
To bitter, angry and scornful
It takes some time to recover
If you ever really do
Or just learn to live with the reality
Facing the pain of losing you
Tomorrow will be a better day
And the next will be even better
Today I soothe my aching heart
By writing you this letter
My memories are all I have
I'll hold them in my heart
Place them where they can't be touched
As my healing begins to start
When I received the news of your leaving
Your departure to places unknown
My heart didn't want to accept it
Although the picture was clearly shown
My mind is intelligent and sharp
Aged with wisdom and knowledge
But this arduous subject of love
Is like being in onerous life's college
I hate that I loved you so much
I'm sorry we ever existed
My desire is that I ignored your attention
And your charming words resisted
But what's done is done, it's over
You can not take life back
Redo it or change the outcome

Or reverse the traveled track
Just allow it to mold and sculpt you
Define your purpose and truth
Experiences in your past
Erudition from your youth
Perspicacity of what is before you
Endeavoring to acquire absolution
Finding peace of mind within
Interminable resolution
For now the resolve is this
I loved you but now your gone
I'm here and I must live
My vivacity carries on
Wherever you are in the universe
I pray your being is well
The end of you has come
How I end only time will tell
But one thing that I am sure of
The lesson I have learned from you
Is that I will never stop being me
No matter what I do
I won't allow my mistakes
My problems, losses or gains
Change who I am inside
Or how warm my heart remains
I will treat everyone that I have loved
Or has loved me thru bad and good
With respect, loyalty and kindness
And the dignity that I should
Your memory serves as a beacon
Of what was, could have been and will be
From regret, anger or uneasiness
I am absolutely free
Goodbye, I will always love you
For that I am not contrite
True love always endures

Love is always right
What is wrong is negative movement
Sometimes we must love from afar
Allow wholesome admiration to exist
But not take us from where we are
I will only remember the goodness
Let the happenings that caused pain dissipate
The happiness, joy and blissfulness
Is all that I will relate
You've paid the ultimate price
It's all that one can do
Farewell to the person I lost
The person that used to be you

LAST NIGHT

Last night I cried because my heart was broken
Trembling lips held words unspoken
Broken spirit lost and confused
No good feelings or reasoning used
I wanted to leave this place and be free
The clouds of comfort carrying me
Drift into dreaming then slowly escape
Deep sweet slumber and never awake
Shattered by words actions and deeds
Cruelty of life and unfulfilled needs
Weary from pain and trying and failing
Emotions being pummeled by hard sharp hailing
Weakened my resolve to continue fighting
No more in small victories delighting
Tears falling down emptying my soul
Drenching my aspirations digging gaping

holes
Overcome by hurt and shame
No longer wanting the victory to claim
Just giving up on every desire
Saying what is the purpose of being a trier
If everything you set your mind to do
Everything you want has always denied you
Why should I bother to try and grab hold
When my grip surely fails and I'm thrown to the cold
I fell into to sleep my body's wages spent
Into deep darkened places where no goodness is meant
To embrace you and fondle you warm softness bring
Where lullabies of damnation and bitterness sing
With prayerful words on my lips I sailed away
Unuttered but hanging on as my misery sway
Clinging for dear life they dug in and clinched
Refusing to let go my tongue they pinched
Making my sleep restless tossed and tumbled
The words of my supplications whispered and mumbled
Determined to reach my Father's ears
For they knew all humble prayers he hears
I awakened mournful limp and weak
Those warring words I still couldn't speak
But it did not matter they were already delivered
Thru the night as my lips and trouble heart quivered

Wrapped in love and soothing the pain
My Father has rescued me again and again
To see another day and negativity erased
Life and love and joy still embraced
My rested soul and comforted heart
Helps me to make a brand new start
No matter how many times I must begin
I'm determined to run the race and win
The flesh is weak but the mind is strong
The heart gets weary but it knows right from wrong
I don't even remember the feelings I felt
Last night as I cried and in prayer knelt
Wiped from my mind and refusing to think
Of the troubles that brought me to the brink
Today is a new day the sun in the sky
A witness to my victory and my help from up high
From where my blessings flow freely like rain
Healing the hurt and cleansing the pain
Thank you Father I will never forget
Your love and compassion your life saving net
But if I do I know you will still
Be there for me my dreams fulfill
For you are like no one else in this place
This universal time and space
Regardless of hardships that will not relent
Others that hurt me without repent
I can always count on you
To hear my cries and see me thru
Even if I'm injured and can not speak
You're busy at work while I'm asleep
I Thank You for shining the sun so bright
And for loving me thru my pain last night

PUZZLE

Are you wondering where love is
Where beauty resides
Are you wondering why goodness
Vanishes and hides
While virtuous beings
Are scattered and few
Why angriness falls
Like the morning dew
Searching for pieces
To fit the mold
Only provided with
what your told
Seeking out edges
With familiar resemblance
Begged of your offspring
Undoubted remembrance
Fitted at angles
Twisted and distorted
Paired with enemies
Deceived and aborted
Gaze at the picture
The masterpiece art
Rearrange in your mind
And take it apart
Put it together
With hands of compassion
Sprinkle with joyous
And temperament ration
Study the lines
Build on desire
Embrace heavens offerings

To lift you up higher
Submit to Creator
Tie self to His tether
Reflect his affection
To put it together
Rebuild this home
To satisfy your needs
Draw power from winds
Sculpture actions and deeds
Repair broken branches
Restore flower and field
Plant trees and water
And fruits they will yield
Abandon the anguish
Replace it with peace
Carve out an opening
For pain to release
Measure the width
And the depth of the ocean
Steady the mountains
To withstand forward motion
Fill the emptiness with
Clean air and presence
Infiltrate the earth
With your natural essence
Formations of wonder
Love soul and heart
Put back together
What has been taken apart

TOUCHED
I'm so wise now
I have been thru so much
Experienced the coldness

And a loving touch
I'm so strong
so lovable So true
Purchased paid for
Sparkling brand new
Uplifted and spiritual
Precious and bold
Unbelievably beautiful
A sight to behold
A treasure of abundant
And plentiful trust
Kindly and loyal
Affirmed and just
Raised in ability
Groomed in strength
Prepared in gracefulness
Proposed at length
Determined and courageous
Empowered and brave
Adorned with love
And my brethren's slave
Related and relating
Approachable face
Enlivened and emboldened
And winning the race
Happy and contented
Peaceful and sound
Feet planted firmly
On the ground
Loved and beloved
Held and beheld
Carried by hands
That never have felled
Carefully watered
Grown with pride
Blissful entitlement

Unable to hide
Touched by the love
The wisdom the power
A grateful aged spirit
A blossoming flower
A song to sing
A melody to play
Golden sunshine
On cloudy day
This I've become
Thru no doing of my own
From the love of God
I have been grown
Touched by his glorious
Amazing heart
Makes me a priceless
Work of art

I AM Pt. 5
I am a Vicious opposer
A protective shield
A sword of insight
I skillfully wield
Intelligence seeker
Scientist of rocket
Mars and moon stones
In my pocket
Dragon slayer
Conveyor of words
Intricate thinking
Lyrical herds
Verbal horizon
On the melodic plain
Calm the savages
Heal the insane

Fight like a Champion
Love strong and deep
Pounce like a tiger
And leopard leap
Ready and willed
I can and I could
Dare you to trifle
Wish that you would
Graceful as an elk
Soaring like an eagle
Standing erect
Distinguished and regal
Born to rule
To lead by example
Voluptuous bountiful
Development ample
Ominous horns
Like a magnificent ram
Proverbial relater
Is who I am

ME
RIGHT NOW IT'S ALL ABOUT ME
Because it has to be
I'm fragile delicate weak
Serenity I seek
Unselfish but self preserved
My sanity reserved
Not indifference but deferred
Solace dimension preferred
Focus on inner being
From chaos catastrophe fleeing
My soul is tired and worn
Tattered from struggle and scorn
Relevant to time and place

Needed air and space
Removed from least resistance
Abiding with spiritual assistance
Welded to harsh reality
Harassing and worrying me
I have to free my mind
Until inner peace I find
Recoiled into bale
In private existence jail
Return I shall indeed
When my innocence is decreed
Wrestle and rift with enmity
Reliance on gracious divinity
Rolling around in grief
Begging for merciful relief
Untied from world at hand
Myself from it demand
Alone not lonely despair
Immersed in respite self care
Don't look from me I'm hiding
Disclose not where I'm residing
Shadows will disappear
And leave my reflection near
Hold on to love for me
Until nature sets me free
I promise to return in spring
When rain falls and bluebirds sing
Please welcome me back to thee
But for now just let me be

CRYBABY
Every time I hear your name
I cry
Every time I hear goodbye
I cry

Every time the birds sing
I cry, I don't know why
When I'm sad and lonely
I cry
When I'm happy and giddy
I cry
The first time you broke my heart I cried
The last time a part of me died
To make things right I know you tried
When you didn't come for me
I cried
The first time you broke your promise
I cried
The tears flowed heavily because
You lied
I put my head on my mother's lap
And she said cry baby cry
It's alright
The first time you said you loved me
I cried
And the first time I heard my baby cry
I cried
And when my grandmother died
I cried
It's the one thing on which I can rely
I can cry

LET
Let not the negative discourage you
Let not the wrong damage your heart
Just let the goodness heal you
And make a brand new start
Let the power embrace you
Be emboldened by the right

Let your strength empower you
And never give up the fight
Let not the evil deceive you
Let not the unrighteous confuse
Let the benevolent conquer bad intentions
The malicious behavior refuse
Let your light shine thru
And help those within your reach
Accept the difficult life lessons
Humility they will teach
Let them also teach you to love
No matter what it takes
Hatred takes away your peace
That heartfelt forgiveness makes
Let all of your virtue praise you
Lest not you praise yourself
Your actions will speak to your character
More precious than any pelf
Let love motivate all movement
If not honorable self keep still
Let not your activity be useless
Your emptiness with substance fill
Live your life with true meaning
Find your purpose and goal
Let go of things with no value
Let partial tendencies become whole
Allow "let" to be a true attribute
Enable it to let positive in
The insightful the praiseworthy the fruitful
Let you be the best you have ever been

GUARDED
Guarded, shadowed
Hidden from love

Expose thyself lest be denied
Joy and magnificence unbounded
Receive thru the wall
Chip away at it's weakened frame
Fly towards me lovebird, fly into my heart
Sword do not guard my soul anymore
I relieve you of your duties
No veil will replace you, only an open window
Breeze, sweep kindness my way
Breathe life into my heart, let the wind shift
Stir my inner self, coax my laughter into the sky
And ricochet off the clouds and tap lightly until
You drum my heart pounding, send showers of rain
To wash away the hurt, light up the electric sky
And allow the light to bring my countenance into view
Let the world see the real me, help me to see clearly
The love at my doorstep and welcome it in
Will me to wrap my arms around it and squeeze it tightly
Let it feel the warmth of my embrace and awaken my soul
Unwrap the bandaged wound so that the salt of the earth can
Heal it's ache. Uncoil the raveled cord of my desperation
And plug it into the source of life, make my heart's desire clear
And apparent and my eyes focus on the beauty of acceptance

Refresh my weary mind so I can find the words to express my
Ocean of feelings and river of emotions, even if the tears should
Fall, steady my feet so I do not drift away. I raise my hands not in
Aggression but as a symbolic pose to let the world know that
I am no longer guarded

SEEK

Seek the answer
The reason why
Seek the things that make you cry
Find a way to figure it out
The painful things that make you shout
Glory days will only come
If you light the darkened way
In the nighttime light a candle
Use the sunlight in the day
Pray for guidance
Down on knees
Until he hears you beg and plead
Father I need you to guide the way
Open up your heart and say
Now is the time I want to know
All that can Lord help me to grow
Help me understand the struggle
The wrong desires that plague my soul
Why the good ones sometimes elude me
And why it feels beyond my control
I need the answers
I'm ready to find

I am not the weakling kind
I have strength adorned by you
I know that it will see me thru
Out of the dark into the night
I know that it will be alright
I have faith that whatever I see
Will be the perfect gift for me
And you will help me understand
What is behind your loving plan
I have hope that never ends
Because my life on you depends
The very things that are yet unseen
Will make me whole and pure and clean
Please soothe my soul and comfort bring
I trust you, your praise I sing
Hear my cry and dry my tears
You've been my source for all these years
I pray that I always remain
The very person you gave this name
Your precious child with tender heart
I have always been a part
Of everything praiseworthy and right
Though sometimes it has been a fight
Now I'm lost and tired out
The will to go on I am without
I have the strength you've given me power
And now I beg this very hour
To give me the will the light and grace
To seek the meaning this time and space
To know where I am where I need to go
I've asked everyone but only you know
Please guide my way to love and peace
Within my heart the hate release
I want to love no matter how wronged
Even if I lose what I feel belonged
To my injured soul I'm low and humble

Please grab my hand if I should stumble
My troubled tears are writing these words
My trembling heart flutters like birds
I'm ready to listen and hear you speak
The answer to that of which I seek
And if the answer breaks my heart
I know that you with amazing art
Will make it beautiful repaired and whole
My refinement is the goal
The only other request I need
Is your command of love the help to heed
Those that love me take not for granted
Those that betray me I forgive
Those that have left me have meant no harm
A wholesome life I want to live
I don't want to hold grudges Or try to repay
Evil for evil, thats the darkened way
I'll love with vigor and appreciate
And needed apologies initiate
Whatever the past I'm letting it go
The pain in my heart Only you truly know
My heart is exposed for all to see
I seek the answers you have for me
I have to listen I know it can come
Thru a loving friend, whoever it's from
I know it originated from you
As I read your word inspired and true
You may tell me to wait be patient be still
And I will obey and do your will
Will beg forgiveness as I make mistakes
And be willing to do whatever it takes
If I've damaged a heart or hurt a friend
I won't ignore or try to pretend
I'll hold them tight and give them my love
For that is the way breathed from above
I'm waiting for a signal or to hear you speak

Please help me find that which I seek

SEEK Pt. 2

I will be honest and open, exposed
The windows to my soul are no longer closed
You see my healing is evading me
I praying to be loosed and set free
If this heart is dark and cold
Please help it heal and my hand hold
Please tell my heart what memories can do
That all I had was given by you
I want to be strong and not give up
You are ready and waiting to fill my cup
With love and trust and healing the sores
Left by the past and slammed closed doors
I couldn't get in, it locked me out
I needed to learn what love is about
Too much time became bitter to taste
And now I desire no more time to waste
Life is so short can be taken in a flash
An illness, violence or a tragic car crash
I don't have the time to feel offended or scorned
The years have tattered, I'm all broken and forlorn
Tell me what's going on what's wrong with my mind
You know me better than anyone I'll find
Please make me understand
That being this way was not the plan
For life to lead me to this place and time
I was suppose to have exactly what's mine

I just need the peace of knowing you're there
I need to feel your love, it doesn't matter where
Don't let anything make my heart cold
I want to feel warmth 'til I'm frail and old
It's wrong it's vile it's inhumane
It's enough to make one go insane
There's no need to be angry and lash out
argue and fuss, scream and shout
I need to let it all go, release it to the sky
Give it a kiss and wave goodbye
You are the best friend I've ever had
There is no reason for me to be sad
I'm hiding afraid to come out and be shown
I'm fearful of hurt and of the unknown
I'll wipe my eyes and try to see, what is truly before my face
What the purpose is for me to be here and take up this space
Clear my mind and start anew and I pray and ask you to make it clear
The answers that I seek about me and why you have brought me here

~~~~~~~~~~~~

The human heart always has hope, even if it is just the tiniest glimmer. It will continue to hope until there is no inkling of a spark. If there is one little spark, hope will hang on.

~RAIN~

It tapped her on the shoulder startling her. As she looked up one hit her on the forehead. Here comes the rain. Kara took out her umbrella and picked up her pace. She was only a few steps from home. She opened the door and stepped inside the house. What a day. It's time to relax . She was tired and hungry. As she prepared herself something to eat, Kara thought about her future. The rain was coming down harder now. She changed her clothes, grabbed her favorite blanket and curled up on the couch to eat her food and listen to the rain. It is like a friend tapping on the window to get your attention. Hello I'm here. It catches a rhythm that dances inside of you, keeping the beat.

THE VILLAGE

The village is quiet
The dark night sky
Is twinkling gently
The moon is high
The air is warm
The trees gently swaying
The wind echoing sounds
Of broken hearts praying
The gentle rain starts
The sound brings relief
It drowns the sorrow
And cleanses the grief
Is there anyone here
That knows where to go
To lay down the burdens
Is there any way to know

What tomorrow brings
What yesterday kept
Who saved her teardrops
As she gently wept
Come sweet tomorrow
Please rescue my mind
I fear that my sanity
Will leave me behind

The Calm Before the Storm
The next morning Kara arose early to prepare for the day. She had an early doctors appointment and she didn't want to be late. The rain had stopped and the morning was clear and bright. This would be her second chemotherapy treatment since she and her doctor had agreed to take this route in fighting her breast cancer. It was difficult but she tried her best to focus on her goal; to fight this, recover and live her life. Her mother and sister had lost the battle but she wasn't giving up. There were so many things she wanted to do and she was going to do them. She walked over to the window, took a deep breath and gazed for a moment to gather herself.

DEAR SKY
I look out of the window and smile at the sky, talk to the clouds and ask them why, why do I wear my heart on my sleeve? Why is it sometimes hard to believe, that everything will eventually be okay, as I look to the sky this beautiful day. Rain will fall

and dampen my skin but it will also quench the thirst within, the sun will burn with intensity, but it's warming rays will always be, the source of light and dry up the rain, heal my wounds and absorb the pain. I'm so grateful to gaze at the smiling moon, when the sun goes down it's never to soon, the dark night soothes the daytime's scorch, it's round and luminous sun lit torch, full and voluptuous, hung on the air, always faithfully humbly there, surrounded by stars that wink at me, twinkle a performance like artistry, as they serenade with heavenly sounds, and sing to me, appreciation abounds. Everything I am and everything I see, empowers, astonishes and blesses me, assures me of love and undying hope, faith and truth in it's broadest scope. Good morning sky, hello dear sun, my long-lived day has just begun, good evening moon, good night stars, as I pray behind these window bars, I bow my head with humility, accepting your honorable plan for me, whatever I say today or do, is accomplished with courage and inspired by you.

The Storm

After chemotherapy Kara was weak and nauseous. A friend met her at the doctor's office to drive her home and to help her. She felt so sick and anger welled up inside of her that she had to endure this. From the beginning she had been determined no to be bitter and ask why me? But this was so hard. Positivity isn't always easy. Especially when it feels like the world is closing in on you, but Kara was determined not to let anger win, even though sometimes it was like battling a beast. On the ride home her friend had to pull over several times. She had been given a receptacle but Kara didn't want to mess up her car. Upon arriving home she helped her into the house and into bed. Her loving friend had been careful not to wear any fragrance that would trigger or worsen Kara's nausea. She told Kara that she would be sitting nearby in the living room if she needed anything. As she lie there in bed she closed her eyes and tried to fight off the beast.

PRAYERFUL (THE BEAST)

Save my soul, save my soul. I'm out of control. Please save my soul.
Soothe your soul out of your control
Haven for the beast power release
Let it be said Let it be done
Soothe yourself lovely one
I want to be saved I pray for peace
Please help me find a haven for the beast
It's power is forceful his grasp is tight
I'm hanging on with all my might
So out of control my mind is everywhere
Racing thoughts over here over there
Tame this beast make it submit
There are no shackles that will fit
It must be wrestled to the ground
Taught to never make a sound
Only when spoken to answer beast
Otherwise let me live in peace

Soothe me hold me rub my back
I need healing from being attacked
This beast within me is controlling my mind
Bringing back things I want to leave behind
Restrain it don't kill it, it deserves to live
It has it's place it's outburst I forgive
It just needs to be tamed and know it's place
It can't indiscriminately show it's face
I can't let it control me I must be in charge
It can't take over my tongue into my vernacular barge
Hold it down while I tranquilize
I need your help I realize
That I can't do this by myself
I need your willingness and loving help
If I can't tame it I'm afraid for me
I will not the same person be
I want to love I want to feel
I want my true heart to be revealed
I want to again feel complete and whole
My prayer is that you save my soul

The Rainbow

Every treatment made her weaker and weaker and she felt herself succumbing to the fatigue. After each appointment she would remind herself, "Just a little bit longer". Her skin changed colors, her mouth and lips were dry and blistered from moisture and wiping. She felt unattractive, frail and tired all of the time. At times she was so miserable she wanted to cry but was too weak and sick. So she just sat and curled up on the couch in her favorite spot with her favorite blanket.

She would go to treatment and see children,

young men and women, older men and women, mothers, grandparents. They all shared a bond of wanting to just get thru this treatment and then the next.

After her treatments were over, Kara had lost a lot of weight along with her hair. But her prognosis was good. "It's time to continue living. "She continued to write in her journal every day. As she sat in her favorite spot on the couch wrapped in her favorite blanket she read the entry she had written the night after she got her diagnosis. It said " All you have to do is............survive."

SURVIVOR

To those who have survived
Amen, to God be the glory
for those who pray for you,
go forth and tell your story.
You're a living testimony,
for all of us to see,
because of your courageous heart,
unending faith have thee
For those who survived the storm
And found a place to hide
Shelter someone in need
A friend in which to confide
Your bravery and steadfastness
Give hope to those who mourn
Give power to the weary
Whose endurance is tattered and torn
Your shine gives light in the darkness
Your loving hand to hold

Helps others stand erect
Empowered, strong and bold

"This story and poem is dedicated to those engaged in the fight against cancer and any other illness you may be fighting. Never Give Up."

~~~~~~~~~~~~~

The human heart always has hope, even if it is just the tiniest glimmer. It will continue to hope until there is no inkling of a spark. If there is one little spark, hope will hang on.

~GRATEFUL~

THE JOURNEY
For so long I carried a burden, It was such a heavy load
It weighed upon my shoulders, as I struggled on the road
I strapped it on my back and carried it to and fro
No matter how hard it weighed on me, I would not let it go
I climbed the highest mountain, I swam the oceans deep
I never let my burden go, no matter how long or steep

I passed some other travelers, along my journey's path
I faced some storms and windy trails, even winter's wrath
Someone who passed would ask me, "May I help you carry it?"
At least stop here and put it down, take time to rest a bit
But I shook my head and told them, I must continue on
And carry this all by myself, my trip is far and long
I can not let you help me, my mind is set in stone
I've decided for my self that I must take this trip alone
My heart has no room for a companion to embrace
There's so much pain inside of me, I do not have the space
There is no way you can help me, of that there is no doubt
If I let you carry it, you may not know the route
I asked my God to help me, I prayed so many times
I felt he had abandoned me and all the fault was mine
Eventually I buckled under the pressure of it all
I felt so low it seemed that I was only two feet tall
I dropped down to my knees and prayed to be set free
of all the pain inside my heart and the anguish drowning me

I cried to God, "I need you, to take this heavy load!
he said, "I tried to take it but you would not let it go.
I'm always here to help you. I never leave your side.
I want so much to help you and to make the ache subside
But you would not accept it, the comfort that I give.
I want you to be happy and enjoy the life you live.
I sent you my direction, a map to guide your way.
I sent you friends and helpers to get you thru each day
And even when you felt alone, someone was always there,
For there are many in your life that treasure you and care.
Accept the help that is given to you. It will only make you strong.
If someone joins you on the way, your trip won't seem so long.
Your journey has a purpose; there is so much life to live.
If you travel properly, forever I will give.
Of course you'll have some baggage as every traveler will
but all must balance out the load and help each other 'til
I take away all the burdens and end the road that leads
to paradise, eternal life and fulfill all travelers' needs.
There will be no need for baggage because

all you need is there.
Until then carry what you need and know I am always there."

SUN

I don't know the reasons why
And I don't pretend that I do
I just sit here and wait to hear
Direction given by you
I know that you love me
I know that I'm here
Only because you say
If there was no special place for me
You would not let me stay
My place is where you say it is
My humble existence is aware
That it matters not where I want to go
If you don't want me there
Sometimes I cry and am brokenhearted
Because of my imperfect mind
But you always treat me with love
And compassion, you are always kind
I try my best to be like you
But usually it is not enough
Trying to reflect you is like
Climbing a mountain, not impossible but tough
I am sad sometimes because I feel lost
Confused and inadequately skilled
Sometimes my actions are misdirected
But with love my heart is filled

Sometimes I feel humiliated
When someone doesn't love me in return
But I know that others are imperfect too
And it is not their intention to spurn
Sometimes I feel like I'm out of place
Like no one understands
What it's like to deal with my life
And all of it's demands
What it is like to have repetitive habits
And thoughts that are trapped in my head
Emotions that control me and won't turn off
Even when I go to bed
But I know that you do
And you are patient with me
Even when I forget to ask
You know my heart and empower me
To accomplish every task
Sometimes I feel blindsided
By developments and reality
But I know someday you will help me accept
And understand in totality
You've given me so much And asked for nothing
But to worship in spirit and truth
There's nothing that I'm not willing to give
I have served you from my youth
And I always will no matter how hard
Be obedient, loyal and trust
That you will always be there for me
For you are gracious, honest and just
I feel your warmth, your precious glow
Shine down on me each day
I never want to forget to thank you
In every possible way
Even with it's problems I welcome the

morning
And Another opportunity to try
Whatever the day brings I will take it on
And never ask you why
You never ask why I sin so much
Or make the same mistakes
You forgive me over and over again
As many times as it takes
You never take the warmth away
The rays you continue to give
The air, the water, the shelter and food
So that I can live
There are so many things that I contend with
But I know I'm not the only one
So grateful that you wake me up each day
To another rising Sun

THE POWER (One)
As you raise your eyes and the light filters thru
Feel the power, the power in you
With outstretched hand and fingertips that are reaching
See the power of life
With head erect and feet placed firmly
Feel the power infusing your skin
Slowly rising, heating vessels
Absorb thru layers and vibrate within
Devour the sustenance your inner self craves
Satisfy the hunger of the starving child
Weed the garden of hopelessness
Keep the lavender from growing wild
Verbalize the refrain

I am not alone, I am not alone, I am not alone
The heart of discontent will drain your strength
render you a helpless weakened shell
Breathe in the stirring breeze that turns the windmill
Absorb the power and empty the well
Drink the water of the nourishing springs
bathe in it's rushing stream
Cleanse the mind of useless chaff
No matter how hopeless it may seem
Sift thru sands washed by ocean's salts
the rising tide bemoan
Sing the melody that echoes in the sky
I am not alone
I am not alone, the power is ready to lift me up it is standing by my side,
willing to give the steps I need determination in my stride
I'm weakened in spirit suffocating from shame searching for someone else to blame
but it matters not the depth of my will
the wind is calmed the water is still
the quiet power of the stars above the moon the sun and it's fire
is at the disposal of it's maker's being that never will falter or tire
Aged with wisdom and embodied with love thunderous claps in the clouds
lightening streaking like ladders of neon, I'm crying your name out loud
Please impart to me the strength I desire
The wisdom I need to escape
The courage I need to endure
The faith I need to believe

And the power to hold my own
I know that I'm not alone
I am not alone

JUBILATION
Jubilation
For creation
Faithful nation
Jubilation
Baby cries
Born again
Without sin
Jubilation
Prayer and repent
Heaven sent
Nature bent
To honor and praise
Voices raise
Beautiful days
Jubilation
Love created
Beings mated
Purpose related
Children conceived
Sins reprieved
Perfection retrieved
Jubilation
Brought back to life
Man and wife
Mother and child
Animals run wild
Free to dance
Life enhance
All creation

Jubilation
Life restored
Praise the Lord
Gray skies blue
I praise you
I honor you
Jubilation
Trees grow tall
Waterfalls
Flowers bloom
No enemies loom
Oceans deeper
Miracle keeper
No frustration
All creation
Jubilation

HONOR

I honor you
For all you do
I praise you too
Worship the true
God is real
Can't you feel
The precious love
From above
No evolving
Problem solving
To not give you
The honor you're due
Disrespectful
So neglectful

Praise his name
Bow down to his throne
Heavens open to visions unknown
Father Provider
Life-giver Inspirer
I'm just a tryer
Have only desire
To honor you
For all you do
For all you have done
The only one
To give your son
So we can live
Our sins forgive
Unmatchable giving
Keeps us living
We try to imitate
The love you initiate
Your power so great
We must appreciate
The gift that's presented
Forgiveness not relented
Can't be earned
Bought or learned
Lawmaker
Promise un-breaker
Promise giver
Always deliver
Loving ways
Days and days
So amazed
By your glory
An endless story
Forever and true
Give praise to you
Give you praise

All our days
We honor you
For all you do

MOMENTUM

Gaining momentum and gathering strength
Prosperous living of any length
Trial and tribulation won't last forever
Hold on relief is near
There is no need for you to tremble
With uncertainty and fear
Pain is glory worn like a badge
An invisible battle scar
A dent in time that gives definition and
Makes you who you are
Never stop moving, never give in
To doubt, uncertainty or denial
This is only a test
Your endurance is on trial
Take the hand of fear itself
Introduce it to your courage & power
Tell it to stay if that it's way
But that it will never devour
Your will to live
Your decision to give
Your happiness, character, your fight
For all you know is standing strong and
erect
and that love is always right
You may be weakened by blows to the head
or
Bent by forceful winds
But love will guide your way to light
As your journey to healing begins

GRATEFUL

Fourteen years old and gone from life
It could have been me
I walked alone from elementary school
The giant park seemed like miles
I was so afraid, so so afraid
She was fourteen years old and now she's gone
Stolen from the street she grew up on
Walking past lonely houses
Wondering where the monsters are hiding
How fortunate am I to be alive
So many have lost the privilege of existence
What will you do with this blessing of breathing
So many things to be sad about
So many problems whistling thru the trees
But laughing and crying exercise the heart
Strengthen the lungs for breathing in and out
Love is a lesson in the reflections of God
The epitome of joy is found in your eyes
So much evil in the world, the true origin we all know
Some deceived, some unaware but it's staring every person
In the face, taunting and torturing the human race
The war against the monsters is fought for us
Praise our protector who fights for us
Show appreciation by living the Light

Be grateful that we do not have to fight
For we are no match for what lurks in the dark
Press your palms like kneading dough
Utter and mumble like a person losing sanity
Bow your head in humble pose thankful for all
For everything I never knew, for everything I know
For anything I didn't do, for everything I did
For everything I never said and anything I said
For all the sins I've been forgiven, for all the love I've held in my heart
For all the hands that I have held, for every love that has held me close
For any sickness I've suffered thru, for every heartache I praise you
For every sigh, every teardrop stain, for all the agony and pain
For things I thought I always wanted, for those I did not receive
For anything I ever had, for the wisdom to believe
For best friends and loved ones near and far, for precious baby boy
For husband, mother, father, sister, brother of my joy
For the gift of hope, the virtue of faith, the strength to not give up
For breath and life and food to eat and water in my cup
For my passion, inner strength, indecision and quirks that baffle some
For earth and nature, sun and rain and the heavens from which they come

For truth and knowledge, the skill to teach,
the humility to learn
For blessings given and the promise of
eternal that I could never earn
For all these things and any I've forgotten
with this imperfect mind
For accepting thanks from me and all the
rest of humankind
For giving me the gift of words poetic,
intelligent or wise
Or just for simple conversation and looking
into someone's eyes
Most importantly for YOU, for your
kindness and your love
Your loyalty ,wisdom, justice and power and
your SON sent from above
For all that's given and all that's taken for
what the future will bring
For you know what is best for me that's why
your praise I sing
For everything I have had in my life and
have learned or will come to know
For the privilege to talk to you and express
how I love You so
For the ability to write this now before the
light of day
With outstretched arms and folded hands I
just want to say
I AM GRATEFUL

~~~~~~~~~

[

www.ingramcontent.com/pod-product-compliance
Lightning Source LLC
Chambersburg PA
CBHW071456040426
42444CB00008B/1370